WHAT YOU
ACCEPT
IS WHAT YOU
TEACH

WHAT YOU ACCEPT IS WHAT YOU TEACH

Setting Standards for Employee Accountability

MICHAEL HENRY COHEN

CREATIVE

HEALTH CARE

MANAGEMENT

ISBN 13: 978-1-886624-76-4
ISBN 10: 1-886624-76-3

Cohen, Michael Henry.
WHAT YOU ACCEPT IS WHAT YOU TEACH : SETTING
STANDARDS FOR EMPLOYEE ACCOUNTABILITY / by Michael
Henry Cohen.
    p. cm.
Includes bibliographical references.
ISBN-13: 978-1-886624-76-4 (pbk. : alk. paper)
    1. Supervision of employees. 2. Performance standards. 3. Behavioral
    assessment. 4. Employees—Coaching of. 5. Problem employees—
    Counseling of. I. Title. II. Title: Standards for employee accountability.
HF5549.12.C645 2006
658.3'14—dc22
        2006030706

Printed and bound in the United States of America

Fourth Printing: October 2008

12 11 10 09 08   8 7 6 5 4

For permission and ordering information, write to:

CREATIVE
HEALTH CARE
MANAGEMENT

Creative Health Care Management, Inc.
1701 American Blvd. East, Suite 1
Minneapolis, MN 55425

chcm@chcm.com
or call: 800.728.7766 or 952.854.9015

www.chcm.com

This book is dedicated to my wife, Jo Ellen Davey Cohen, the love of my life, and to the family that we have created.

A NOTE TO THE READER

Management is an art, not a science. It's a practice. There are no simple answers or magic formulas for success. I do have a distinct point of view, and I present it in a very forthright manner. I may say some things that you flat-out disagree with. That's okay. Through the free marketplace of competing ideas, the truth marches forward.

I hope you will find this book thought-provoking and insightful, but above all practical. My intent is to provide you common-sense, down-to-earth advice that you can immediately apply when faced with a performance-management challenge.

Ultimately, you will have to find your own way and learn from trial and error what works best for you. If this book helps you in the process, then I have accomplished my objective. Good luck and enjoy the journey!

Michael Henry Cohen

CONTENTS

ACKNOWLEDGEMENTS

I am exceedingly grateful for my content experts, who reviewed drafts of this book and rendered insightful, practical advice on how to improve upon it. They are Diane Dassow, Shirley Heintz, RN, Susan Kinsman, RN, Mindy Malecki, Kathleen Prunty, Evelyn Schnitzer and Rhonda Stuart. I also want to thank Brenda Grover, who transcribed raw material from dictation into an organized, accessible final draft; Karen Lundquist, who was a joy to work with and whose editing of this book was thoroughly professional; and Chris Bjork, my direct link to Creative Health Care Management, for his wise counsel and strong advocacy throughout the duration of this project.

It is unkind to shield people from the consequences of their own behavior. In doing so, we teach them they are inadequate and weak. When we give in to irresponsible behavior by excusing it or sympathizing with it, we condone and foster spoiled, law-unto-self conduct. And if we give up—by ignoring or tearing into them—we undermine their motivation to improve. The doctrine *Don't give up and don't give in*, tempered with love, comes from responsible, disciplined living.

Stephen R. Covey

THE PURSUIT OF MEDIOCRITY IS ALMOST ALWAYS SUCCESSFUL

To exist without limits is to act without values. A manager who does not establish boundaries by upholding reasonable standards of conduct inevitably invites chaos, shoddiness and despair. While passivity in response to employee wrongdoing results in no immediate harm and confers no direct hurt, it creates a permissive work environment in which destructive behaviors are tolerated, even encouraged.

What you accept is what you teach. If you don't reinforce and hold everyone accountable for outstanding performance, you compromise your organization's mission, sabotage your department's reputation and diminish your own credibility. The marginal employee is, after all, a reflection on you.

There are two distinct marks of great leaders. First, they are fired by values and stay true to them no matter what the consequences. Second, they generally believe that betraying these values would constitute the greatest of moral failures. Give up, they say to themselves, and both complacency and mediocrity triumph. Stand firm, and you have the power to inspire other leaders and to transform organizations.

Unfortunately, we are living in a very litigious society. Employees are quick to sue at the slightest provocation. As a result, many managers act as if they are walking on eggs. They are too tentative. They are afraid to take a stand for fear of offending an employee. They believe that they will not be supported by their human resource department, their manager or upper level leaders. They feel that they are held hostage to staff shortages, and they know how difficult it could be to replace someone. Therefore, too many managers are lowering their standards, tolerating minimum acceptable performance or dysfunctional employee behaviors. They are settling for mediocre results.

When You Don't Hold Employees Accountable

The three most important decisions you will ever make as a manager are whom you hire, whom you promote, and whom you allow to remain on your team. You are only as good as your weakest link, and unless you have the best players in the most strategic positions, your team will never realize its full potential. Therefore, if you have an employee who lacks the will or skill to effectively perform his job, the worst things that you can do are:

- wait for the employee to eventually see the light and do the right thing—and then get upset when he doesn't

- avoid unpleasant confrontations, believing that frank and truthful feedback will damage the relationship

- ignore, deny, rationalize or minimize performance deficiencies that need to be addressed

- fear that confronting the employee will only make the person more defensive and make the situation worse

- assume that any corrective action will not be supported by upper level management or by the human resource department (so why bother if your intervention will be overturned?)

- believe that just because an employee is technically competent, you have to accept dysfunctional behaviors and negative attitudes

- tolerate excuses, thereby preventing people from accepting the reality that they own the problem

- fail to clearly state your expectations for change, monitor and evaluate results, communicate progress and mete out consequences when necessary

Holding someone accountable need not be negative, abusive or demeaning for the individual involved. Establishing clear goals, measuring them, recognizing achievement and holding people accountable are the essence of effective performance management.

Some employees have never received an honest appraisal in their life. No manager has ever leveled with them about their marginal performance. They have been conditioned to think that their performance is acceptable because no one has ever said otherwise. They are satisfied with the quality of their work. It's not the employee's problem. It is your customers' problem when they are victims of the employee's incompetence. It is the co-worker's problem when they are subjected to the employee's counterproductive behavior. It is *your* problem. After all, if you don't hold the employee accountable for performance improvement, your manager might hold *you* accountable for customer complaints, a decline in employee morale, increased turnover, a loss of your best employees and a general reduction of performance quality.

The employees you hold accountable for poor performance never cause you as much trouble as those you don't hold accountable but should. If you don't deal forthrightly with incompetent or uncooperative employees, you are giving tacit approval for their unacceptable behavior to continue. Your valuable employees will begin to wonder, "Why should I put in a full day's work for an honest day's pay when this co-worker is demonstrating laziness, incompetence and rudeness?" Good employees would rather work shorthanded for a reasonable period of time than have to regularly deal with an incompetent or toxic co-worker. If you pit a good person against a bad system, the bad system wins almost every time. Good employees leave bad systems and go elsewhere. And they should. This is the marketplace in action.

If you overlook the misbehavior of the few, you will lose the respect of the many. And if you avoid the truth about poor performance in order to keep your employees from being hurt, you end up hurting them even more. As a result of your self-imposed impotence, you will begin to develop resentment, if not contempt, toward your difficult employees. You will begin to ignore them, withhold everyday pleasantries, fail to acknowledge any achievements and strengths, talk negatively about them to others or secretly hope that they quit.

You may be asking yourself how other employees will *know* that you are holding the poor performer accountable. Obviously, you cannot publicize your private conversations. But inevitably employees will find out that you have confronted the person because one of three events will occur:

- The employee will tell everyone who is willing to listen what transpired during your "confidential" coaching sessions and will probably distort everything that you said. Co-workers may feign sympathy for this employee, but they will be secretly delighted that you finally confronted the issue.

- Co-workers will begin to observe positive behavioral change in the employee, and they will assume that this is a direct result of your intervention. You will gain credibility within your department for facilitating improvement in the person's performance.

- If no positive behavior change is evident and the performance deficiency is significant, the employee will ultimately be discharged. This will provide you the opportunity to select and train a new employee who has the willingness and capacity to meet your expectations.

Practice Tough Love

You must believe in and practice tough love with your employees to be an effective manager. The *tough* part of this equation is that you are ever vigilant in pursuit of excellence. You have the courage to demand the best of your employees, but in the process you:

- maintain high standards for everyone and display no favoritism or preferential treatment

- serve as a positive role model for the attitudes and behaviors expected of employees

- provide recognition for achievement and celebrate individual and team accomplishments

Do not be afraid to use the power inherent in your position to hold employees accountable for achieving outstanding results. There is a myth that power or organizational politics is nasty business, that being power-conscious is destructive and implies a desire to manipulate or control employees. In fact, power is neither good nor bad. Power is neutral. Simply defined, power is the capacity to get things done, and it is attained by your ability to gain the support and trust of coworkers. You accomplish this by providing resources to facilitate others' success, which, in turn, makes it easier to receive assistance toward the accomplishment of your goals.

Knowing how to get things done and holding employees accountable for what they are being paid to accomplish are in no way destructive. If you use your position power to achieve positive results through ethical means, then having clout to make things happen is not only desirable, it is a precondition for success.

Why do you want to be a manager? Given all of the potential stress and conflict associated with the role, there exists only one sound motivation for wanting the job: You want to place yourself in a pivotal position to make a positive difference, to leave the campsite cleaner than it was when you found it.

If you are reluctant to exercise your legitimate power for fear of not being liked or because you don't want to offend someone's feelings, in the long run you will be neither liked nor respected by employees. You are being paid to run a department and to safeguard its critical organizational functions. If the work team you are managing does not adhere to the accepted standards of conduct, service or production, at some point you may find yourself without a department to manage.

The *love* part of this equation is that your employees know you believe in them, are vested in their success and will do everything within reason to help them meet your lofty expectations. You will run interference for your employees, support them under fire, watch their backs, access resources for them, speak on their behalf and remove system barriers that impede their success. You are their ally and their representative to upper level management.

But your support does not mean unconditional acceptance of everything they do. You should *never* compromise on your vision, values and standards. Your department's quality of performance either gets better or it gets worse. It never stays the same. And unless you demand continuous improvement, your employees' quality of performance and team morale will inevitably decline.

Remember, you don't enhance an individual's self-esteem by lowering your standards, enabling the person to meet minimum expectations. You develop and reinforce a person's self-esteem when you maintain high standards, provide a supportive environment that facilitates the person's success, and recognize achievement, even if the individual's improvement comes in incremental steps.

Finally, there is another myth that the closer you get to employees on a personal basis and the more involved you become in their personal problems, the more likely you will get cooperation from them. This notion is false.

Don't get so close to employees that you can be expected to "understand" when they don't effectively perform their jobs. You need to maintain a certain psychological distance and objectivity to remain the cool, calm problem solver necessary to execute your management responsibilities.

Don't turn a deaf ear when an employee wants to share a personal problem that may be negatively impacting her work. Listen to her and empathize with what she is going through. But you are her manager, not her psychologist. Remind the employee that while you are sensitive to her situation, your first priority is to ensure that the work gets done and that you hold all employees accountable for their conduct and the impact it has on the work team.

Make whatever accommodations you deem appropriate and offer the resources of an employee assistance counselor if available. But don't get sucked into or held hostage to the employee's personal problems. You will only enable her marginal performance, and you will lose credibility with other employees who *are* doing their jobs in spite of their own personal issues.

Notes:

Authority: The ability to influence or persuade resulting from one's knowledge, experience, personal credibility or position power; confidence derived from skill and practice; firm self-assurance.

To hold someone accountable: entrust, charge, put under obligation, enjoin, expect, make mandatory, enforce rules, exact compliance.

To hold oneself accountable: to make it one's duty, fulfill an obligation, keep a covenant; have a moral sense of conscience; to answer the call, be engaged, act or play one's part; obey.

The American Heritage College Dictionary and
Roget's International Thesaurus

YOUR RIGHTS AS A MANAGER

There have been attempts over the years to democratize work and to flatten the organizational chart. The organizational pyramid, however, remains the most pervasive and dominant fact of organizational life. Hierarchical arrangements of people, as represented by an organizational chart, are necessary for work to be accomplished. As a species, we form hierarchies spontaneously. Someone must be in charge before anything can even be started.

When an employee accepts a job to work within your department, he signs his name to an unwritten psychological contract, a covenant of employment that in return for pay and benefits he agrees to:

- exercise self-control, adhere to standards of professional conduct and acknowledge that these rules of civil behavior are fair and good for the organization

- do what it takes to get the job done, make a sacrifice through contribution, achieve positive outcomes
- demonstrate loyalty to you, the work team and the organization
- submit willingly to your authority as a manager to coach, appraise, discipline, assign work and schedule time off

As manager, you are a legitimate authority figure in the employee's work life. The employee does not have to like you personally. But he does need to legitimize and sanction your right to tell him what to do, and he does need to treat you with respect and courtesy. In the military, when you salute an officer, you are not saluting the person, you are saluting the rank. It is the role and status that must be respected and honored regardless of personal feelings toward the officer.

In fact, you have the right to ask an employee to do *anything* and to expect that he will do it in a competent manner providing that your expectation is (1) job related, (2) communicated in advance, (3) reasonable, (4) safe, legal, and ethical and (5) nondiscriminatory. This chapter describes in detail these rights and your responsibilities that accompany them.

Your Expectations Must Be Job Related

You have the right to ask an employee to perform any task providing that your expectation is part of the nature, function and scope of that person's job. The expectation is described somewhere in the employee's job description. It is consistent with the organization's mission, vision and values. You are not asking the employee to do something out of personal whim or fetish, or because you simply don't like the person. What you're asking the employee to do is based on *business necessity*. The task must be carried out in order to satisfy the customer, maintain the reputation of the organization, uphold the morale of the department or comply with legal and regulatory mandates.

If ever there is a challenge as to whether the expectation is job related your best defense is a current job description. Make certain, therefore, that each employee *has* a job description and that it serves as an accurate summary of the employee's responsibilities. When you must defend your management action, the job description is the source from which all blessings flow.

To ensure that your expectations are job related, think about what you want your customers to say about your department, the results you want to have accomplished and the values you want demonstrated. Also identify the hills that you are willing to die on—those specific employee performance expectations that are not negotiable.

Know what you stand for and will never compromise regardless of circumstances. If you stand for nothing, you are willing to accept anything. It's not a *right* to work within your organization. Nobody is *entitled* to a job. It is a privilege to be employed, and with this privilege comes specific responsibilities and conditions of employment.

If you have 101 priorities, all of them important, you have no priorities. You have no focus. One definition of leadership is "the effective management of attention." Because you don't have enough resources to be great at everything, you must select very carefully what you want employees to focus on. Regardless of job classification, there are four key results areas, driven by business necessity, for which every employee should be held accountable: technical competence, customer service, effective teamwork and fiscal responsibility.

Technical Competence

Every employee must be knowledgeable, skillful and re-sourceful. The goal here is that every employee should strive to be *cutting edge* in his field of expertise. Nobody, regardless of age or length of employment, should be allowed to rest on his laurels. Nobody should be permitted to practice OJR (On-the-Job Retirement). Once a person stops learning or is no longer challenged, he gets demotivated and habitu-ated. Therefore, you should create a *learning culture* in which everyone is engaged in continuous quality improvement.

In pursuit of this goal, at the end of every annual per-formance appraisal, you should ask each employee the fol-lowing question:

> "This time next year, what will you know that you don't know now, and how will you ap-ply this knowledge or skill to the benefit of the department?"

You and the employee should informally negotiate a *stretch* learning objective, a goal that will move the em-ployee out of her comfort zone. After establishing the an-nual goal, discuss existing resources that will facilitate the employee's success in accomplishing the result. Set the em-ployee up for success through training and development, coaching and mentoring.

Outstanding Customer Service

Everyone has either external or internal customers. If it is not your job to directly serve the external customer, then it is your job to serve those who do. The goal here is not to merely meet customers' expectations but to exceed—*wow*—them whenever possible. To accomplish this result, every employee must know the answers to these questions:

- Who are my customers?

- What are my customer's needs and expectations? What are the criteria by which the customer evaluates me? What does the customer value most in terms of the services I provide?

- What specifically should I say and do to meet or exceed my customer's expectations?

It is important to recognize that *quality of customer service is a perception issue*. If customers do not perceive that they have been well served, then by definition they have *not* been well served. Quality is whatever the customer says it is.

If enough customers say negative things about one employee, they all can't be wrong, crazy or out to get the employee. If there exists a pattern of negative customer feedback, the employee should be held accountable for the negative impressions being made. You don't need to directly observe the employee in action to know there's a problem. Customer feedback serves as the evidence. It doesn't matter *how* the employee is achieving negative impressions. The fact that enough credible customers are complaining is sufficient to hold the person accountable.

Effective Teamwork

There is no room for a prima donna or a lone ranger within your department. You probably don't have enough staff as it is. Therefore, you have a right to expect that every employee is constructive and collaborative with other team members within and between job classifications, shifts and departments. It also means that every employee should consider it a top priority to keep you satisfied with his work and to maintain a positive relationship with you.

At the very least, being an effective team player means:

- coming prepared to work as the schedule requires
- demonstrating a strong work ethic
- talking directly to the person with whom there is a problem
- avoiding continuous griping, dumping, backbiting and tattling
- becoming a part of the solution to problems identified

Fiscal Responsibility

It is everyone's job to look for ways to make or save money for the department and organization. This includes:

- utilizing materials and supplies prudently
- taking care of equipment
- putting things away
- locking things up so that they don't disappear
- not abusing meal or break times
- remaining goal focused and task oriented on paid productive work time
- identifying creative ways to stay within the budget

It is in everyone's economic self-interest to do these things, because without a margin, there is no mission—let alone merit increases, perks or job security.

Your Expectations Must Be Communicated

You can't hold someone accountable for an expectation that has not been communicated. The employee can't read your mind. Therefore, it is your responsibility to provide prompt and unambiguous answers to these critical questions:

- What are the key results areas to be achieved?
- What are the indicators of success? What does it *look like* to effectively perform the job? (Performance standards must be measurable, observable or verifiable in some way.)
- What monitoring and evaluation system will you use?
- How should the employee perform the job? What policies, procedures, protocols, oral traditions, regulatory mandates or industry practices must be respected?
- What resources exist (or don't exist) to facilitate the employee's success? You can't hold someone accountable for something she has no control over.

Once you are in a position to observe the employee's performance, you then must offer constructive feedback:

- How well is the employee meeting your expectations? There should never be any surprises or new issues raised during the employee's year-end performance appraisal. This smacks of managerial malpractice. Evaluation should be an ongoing process. An employee's strengths and deficiencies should be communicated in a timely manner.
- If the employee is not effectively performing his job, what must he start or stop doing in order to meet

your expectations? The more specific and behaviorally concise your instructions are, the better.

- When do you want to see these changes made?

- Does the employee understand that improvement must be consistently demonstrated over a sustained period of time?

- What is the magnitude of the performance deficiency? What are the consequences for not making these changes? Could failure lead to discharge?

- What are the rewards if positive change is indicated?

- When will you provide feedback relative to the employee's performance improvement? High-maintenance employees require more structured and regular feedback. When necessary, conduct quarterly performance appraisals to document the employee's work quality or, if necessary, to build a case for termination.

You must also *document what you have communicated* to secure the necessary support from your manager and the human resource department. This documentation should take the form of:

- anecdotal records of your conversations with the employee

- department meeting minutes that summarize communicated expectations for all team members

- e-mail correspondence

- policy and procedural manuals

- training documents that indicate how employees should perform certain tasks

- new employee orientation checklists that document the prerequisite knowledge and skills to effectively execute specific responsibilities

This documentation could become a critical record in a wrongful discipline or discharge allegation. The complete document will prove that you not only communicated your expectations in a clear, concise and timely manner, but that you also let employees know the consequences of their actions.

Your Expectations Must Be Reasonable

Reasonable is a relative and subjective term. What you consider to be reasonable and what the employee deems reasonable might be considerably different. Criteria do exist, however, to objectively judge whether your expectations are fair and reasonable:

- *If other employees within the same job classification* are able to perform this task in a satisfactory manner given the same constraints and limitations, then why is this person any different? Your expectation, therefore, is reasonable.

- *If you have effectively performed this job* given the same working conditions, you know that your expectations are probably reasonable.

- *If the employee is degreed, licensed or certified* by a legitimate academic institution, your expectations are reasonable because they are in line with professional standards and mandates.

- *If you have removed all of the significant system barriers* that serve as an impediment to the employee's success (the person has sufficient space, equipment, materials and supplies, cooperation from other departments), then it is reasonable to assume the employee should be able to meet your expectations.

* *If you have provided sufficient training and development* to set up the employee for success, then it is reasonable to expect that the employee will perform in a competent manner.

Your Expectations Must Be Safe, Legal and Ethical

You cannot require an employee to do something that will put her or someone else at risk physically, legally or professionally. In fact, if asked to do something unsafe, illegal or unethical, an employee has not only the right, but also the *responsibility* to refuse your request.

You and the employee, however, might have different interpretations of what is legal, ethical and safe. For this reason, you should discuss with employees on a proactive basis what situations might place them at risk and explore the constructive responses to these questionable situations.

Ensure that all employees are aware of your organization's formal grievance procedure, corporate compliance policy, chain of command and problem solving protocols. These checks and balance systems provide employees the opportunity to access objective, third-party resources to mediate conflict or interpret rights and responsibilities. As a manager, you should not be threatened or defensive about these employee resources. A fair employee appeal process, for example, can support you when you make an unpopular decision or execute a corrective action that is in the best interest of the organization.

Attain working knowledge of your organization's personnel policies, procedures and guidelines. Apprise your manager and the human resource department of sensitive employee-relations issues. By keeping others in the loop, you will increase the likelihood that, if challenged, your decisions will be upheld.

Your Expectations Must Be Nondiscriminatory

This is not a book about employment law, but it is important that you have at least a working knowledge of the following laws:

- Title VII of the 1964 Civil Rights Act prohibits employment discrimination based on race, color, religion, sex and national origin.

- The Age Discrimination in Employment Act of 1967 (ADEA) covers age discrimination in employment for individuals who are 40 years of age or older.

- Title I and Title V of the Americans with Disabilities Act (ADA) prohibit employment discrimination against qualified individuals with disabilities who work in the private sector and in state and local governments.

- Sections 501 and 505 of the Rehabilitation Act of 1973 prohibit discrimination against qualified individuals with disabilities who work in the federal government.

- The Civil Rights Act of 1991, as well as other legislation, provides monetary damages in cases of intentional employment discrimination.

- The United States Department of Labor Occupational Safety and Health Administration (OSHA) ensures workers' safety and health.

- The National Labor Relations Board (NLRB) administers the National Labor Relations Act by conducting elections to determine whether or not employees want union representation and by investigating and remedying unfair labor practices by employers and unions.

- The United States Department of Fair Labor Standards Act (FLSA) establishes minimum wage, overtime pay, record keeping and child labor standards affecting full-time and part-time workers in the private sector and in federal, state and local governments.

- The Family and Medical Leave Act (FMLA) grants family and temporary medical leave under certain circumstances.

- While sexual orientation is not a protected class under federal law, some states have adopted laws to protect employees from discrimination based on sexual orientation.

- Each state has its own workers' compensation laws.

- Each state has its own unemployment compensation laws.

State and local law will provide additional employee protections, and you should familiarize yourself with the various agencies that handle employment-related claims.

The intent of these employee protections is to ensure that all management decisions such as hiring, promoting, scheduling, assigning work, appraising, disciplining and discharging are based upon a person's quality of performance, not personal prejudice. To ensure that you are effectively managing performance within a culturally diverse workplace, you must communicate a commitment to fair treatment, identify standards of performance that apply to everyone and hold everyone accountable to rules of civil behavior. You should also conduct a personal self-evaluation to identify any potential bias. Make certain that you engage in the following practices:

- Deal with employees and situations on an individual basis, recognizing that each person is unique. Avoid stereotyping.

- Become aware of language that has a questionable racial, ethnic or sexual connotation. Insensitive or inflammatory remarks should not be tolerated.

- Avoid patronizing and tokenism toward any group. Hold everyone equally accountable to high standards of performance and conduct.

You can't possibly be an expert in all areas of labor and civil rights law, but you must be aware of the specific acts and words that will get you in trouble. Whenever you are uncertain about the legal implications of your decisions, contact your human resource department for advice and consent. This department should be considered a resource for staff at any and all levels.

Another myth that contributes to self-doubt and inaction is that you must be absolutely fair with employees to earn credibility and be effective. But the terms *absolute* and *fair* are at odds with one another. *Absolute* suggests without exception, unconditional, not to be questioned. *Fair*, on the other hand, is a relative and subjective concept meaning dependent on circumstance or interconnected with a particular situation (not absolute).

Should you strive to be fair and consistent in the administration of organizational and personnel policies? Yes. But on occasion, you have to make (and are being paid to make) judgment calls based upon your perception of events. It is impossible to quantify or objectify your perceptions. However, just because you can't count something doesn't mean that it does not exist or is not important. Your perceptions, interpretations and conclusions matter and shouldn't be discounted by employees just because they are inherently subjective. Your perceptions matter because you are the manager.

Lower your standards and nothing
will ever disappoint you.

———————————————

Author Unknown

DEVELOPING PERFORMANCE STANDARDS AND EVALUATING OUTCOMES

The previous chapter highlighted the importance of communicating your expectations in a timely and behaviorally concise manner. Employees must know what competence, customer service or teamwork *looks like*. What are the indicators of success? What are the standards by which employees will be evaluated and held accountable?

A performance standard is a completed objective that is observable, quantifiable or verifiable. If you can't *measure it, see it, hear it, or otherwise verify its existence*, you can't evaluate it. A performance standard is a statement that describes how you know when a job is well done or when the outcome meets a targeted goal. Questions associated with performance standards include the following:

- Is there a certain way in which the job should be performed?

- Are there time frames that must be met?

- Does a certain amount or degree of quality need to be achieved?

- What are the specific results that must be achieved?

Standards must be communicated to employees in an understandable and accurate way as a realistic description of the performance *quality, quantity, accuracy, thoroughness, timeliness or cost effectiveness.* But they should not be developed and communicated in an autocratic or arbitrary manner. You will never achieve voluntary compliance and enthusiasm for your performance standards if you approach employees in a "Now hear this" style, such as:

"These are your standards. You will like them, and they will be good for you. You will be held accountable to these standards, and there will be consequences if you don't comply with them!"

A better approach is to initially develop a draft of performance standards and review them with staff. Utilize your employees on a consultative basis. Elicit their input by asking the following questions:

- Are these standards practical and realistic?

- Do these standards represent the best practices of individuals within our department, organization or industry?

- How can we fine-tune these standards so that all employees know what is expected of them and understand the criteria by which they will be evaluated?

Exercises to Develop Teamwork Standards

Most organizations publish mission, vision and value statements. They are all very well written and bring a tear to the eye. But all too often, there is a huge disconnect between employees' actual conduct and the official organizational philosophy. This condition breeds cynicism among those employees whose behavior is consistent with organizational values.

Buddha said, "To know and not to do is not to know." All employees *say* they value teamwork, for example, but do they know what they should *do* to maintain a positive, service-driven work environment? Do all employees have the same understanding of what it means to effectively communicate with one another, solve problems and manage conflicts? Before you can hold employees accountable for effective teamwork, you must first establish clear and concise standards. To accomplish this objective, ask employees to complete the following lists:

1. Describe the characteristics of the best team player with whom you have ever worked.

2. Describe the characteristics of the co-worker from hell.

Issues to consider when developing best and worst teamwork practices may include how an employee demonstrates her:

- Attitude, work and service ethic

- Relationship with members of different shifts, work units and job classifications

- Communication with manager(s)

- Conflict management and problem-solving

- Commitment to continuous learning/technical competence

- Welcoming of new employees

By identifying the best and worst teamwork practices, employees are, in effect, handing you a mandate to recognize indicators of effective teamwork and to hold them accountable for constructive conduct. You can also integrate these standards into your performance appraisal and new employee orientation process. (See examples of best and worst teamwork practices on pages 37 and 38 respectively.)

Cooperrider (2000, 113) provides five additional exercises that involve employees in the development of teamwork standards:

1. Acknowledge anything that you have seen co-workers do to enhance the overall quality of cooperation and communication within the team.

2. Discuss what should be preserved about our values, traditions and best practices even as we look for ways to improve team functioning.

3. What do you value most about yourself, the nature of the work you do or the work of the team?

4. Identify three wishes to heighten the quality and health of our work team. What can we do to make our jobs easier, more satisfying and effective?

5. Describe peak experiences or high points within the team when co-workers went above and beyond their duty to exceed team members' expectations. Recall specific examples when our mission and values truly become realized through our words and deeds.

An Exercise to Develop Customer Service Standards

Don't assume all employees understand what is meant when you say, "I expect that your customer interactions will always be courteous and respectful." Those employees practicing TDC (Thinly Disguised Contempt) toward customers probably believe they *already are* acting in a professional, dignified manner. Therefore, you must develop consistent, clearly understood measures of performance and hold everyone accountable to them.

Customer service is a performing art. An employee is onstage playing a role and should never break character. Every time she comes into contact with a customer, there exists a "Moment of Truth" in which she is being sized up as if she's being interviewed. She can never let her guard down. What are the Moments of Truth in your department?

1. Utilizing the form on page 35, identify the most critical Moments of Truth that occur within your department: those key customer-employee interactions when a service is being rendered and an impression is being made. For example, in a hospital emergency department, at least five Moments of Truth exist when a customer is assessing the quality of service. They are, in sequential order, as follows:

   - The registration clerk interaction (first contact)
   - The triage nurse assessment
   - The wait to be seen by a physician
   - The patient examination and treatment
   - The patient discharge (last contact)

Within each Moment of Truth, the goal is to make customers feel welcome and comfortable, to earn their respect and appreciation. If employees effectively manage each Moment of Truth, customers will proceed from one interaction to the next with confidence that the emergency department is a safe, secure, professional and caring environment.

The luck of the draw—which particular employee happens to be taking care of a customer—should not determine the quality of service rendered. You want to hold everyone accountable for consistent and predictable standards of conduct.

2. For each Moment of Truth, identify the customer's needs and expectations (the criteria the customer is using to judge the quality of service).

3. Identify what all employees should consistently say and do to meet or exceed the customer's expectations within each Moment of Truth.

4. Identify what all employees should *never* say and do that would create a negative impression.

Include scripts and nonverbal behaviors that communicate employees' attitude and demeanor. Remember, customers form impressions of employees within the first six seconds of an interaction. There is no second chance to create a positive first impression. It's not just *what* the employee says that matters, but *how* he says it: the speed, volume, tone of voice and visual cues such as eye contact, facial expressions, attire and overall poise.

5. During each Moment of Truth, things that are outside an employee's control can and will go wrong. Identify what the employee can say and do to rectify the situation or make the customer feel that she has been heard, understood and taken seriously.

An Exercise to Develop Standards for Four Key Results Areas

Chapter 2 listed four key results areas driven by business necessity for which everyone should be held accountable. Another practical exercise that gets employees involved in the development of their own performance standards is to ask them to recommend specific conduct for each of the key results areas:

1. List the five most important behaviors or activities that demonstrate a co-worker's commitment to technical competency.

2. List the five most important behaviors or activities that demonstrate a co-worker's commitment to customer service.

3. List the five most important behaviors or activities that demonstrate a co-worker's commitment to teamwork.

4. List the five most important behaviors or activities that demonstrate a co-worker's commitment to fiscal responsibility.

Collect employees' written input, summarize the responses under each category and share at a team meeting. After discussion, ask employees to sign off on these standards indicating that they understand what is expected of them, that they affirm each expectation is reasonable, job related and within their control to meet and that they agree to be held accountable for displaying these behavioral characteristics. Employees who participate in the development of these standards are more likely to enthusiastically and effectively operationalize your organization's customer service values.

MOMENT OF TRUTH:

Customer Expectations: _____

_____

_____

_____

_____

_____

What employee should do or say to meet or exceed customer expectations (include nonverbal behavior as well, such as body language, tone of voice, etc.):

_____

_____

_____

_____

_____

What employee should *never* do or say that would create a negative impression:

_____

_____

_____

_____

_____

Things that can go wrong and what employee should do:

_____

_____

_____

_____

_____

Discuss ambiance issues that may impact customer perceptions: cleanliness, noise level, desktop neatness, lighting, quality of reading material and other positive diversions in customer waiting areas, etc.:

_____

_____

_____

_____

_____

Examples of Best Teamwork Practices

- Employees have positive things to say about their jobs and the people with whom they work.

- They are good at what they do. They are skillful and resourceful.

- They make work fun. They have a good sense of humor.

- They are focused on how they can make things better. Rather than complain or whine, they look for answers.

- They are open to change. They are adaptable and flexible.

- They build people up rather than tear them down. They make those around them feel more motivated, important and effective in their work.

- They are enthusiastic. They possess a high level of energy in pursuit of positive outcomes.

- They prefer peace over conflict.

- They maintain self-control during frustrating situations.

- They enjoy learning and welcome challenging situations.

- They work well with a wide variety of people. They have a high tolerance for diverse cultures, personalities, work styles and perspectives.

- They come to work as scheduled, prepared for work. They follow the published call-in procedure.

- When finished with their own work, they offer assistance to others in need of help without being asked.

- If they have conflicts with co-workers, they talk to (not about) them at the earliest possible opportunity, and they remain cool, calm and collected. They are direct, honest and respectful.

- They acknowledge co-workers when they enter a room. They exchange pleasantries when they come into contact with others. They say "please" and "thank you." They can be friendly without being friends. They say "hello" in the morning and "goodbye" in the afternoon. They conduct themselves in a professional and courteous manner.

Examples of Worst Teamwork Practices

- Employees do as little as possible to get by. They are frequently heard saying, "It's not my job" or "I can't help you."

- They are always late, or they arrive unprepared for work.

- They take extra long breaks or lunches.

- They constantly argue over assignments.

- They question every decision.

- They complain incessantly.

- They frequently find fault and make negative comments about the department and organization.

- They are very judgmental of co-workers, especially of new employees. They never offer to help others or volunteer.

- They flaunt their strong technical skills and are very condescending toward co-workers with lesser skills or experience.

- They gossip and tattle on co-workers.

- They don't own their mistakes.

- They get very defensive when given honest, respectful performance feedback.

- They are concerned only with what's best for themselves, their own shift or their own work unit.

- They bring personal problems to work.

- They are subject to extreme mood swings.

- They don't pick up after themselves.

- They are rigid regarding change.

- They are very thin-skinned and are often looking for ways to be offended.

- They are slow and unable to keep up with the pace.

- They are unwilling or unable to perform specific tasks, forcing others to pick up the slack.

- They are overly critical of new employees: They ignore them or refuse to answer their questions. They are quick to criticize, reluctant to credit. When approached by a new employee in need of help, they demonstrate nonverbal behaviors that communicate "I'm too busy—figure it out for yourself." *They eat their young.*

- They argue with co-workers in eyesight or earshot of others.

- They use customers as a sounding board to criticize co-workers or other departments.

- If they have problems with co-workers, they yell, swear, interrupt, call them names or engage in threatening words or actions.

- They constantly gripe and dump about work frustrations. They refuse to attend or participate at meetings that are designed to address employee concerns and then complain *after* the meeting about problems that they are not willing to help solve.

Examples of Best Customer Service Practices

- When you meet a customer for the first time, smile, establish eye contact and introduce yourself by name and position.

- If appropriate, ask the customer how to pronounce his or her name or what he or she would like to be called. Otherwise, *Sir* or *Ma'am* can and should be used to address your customers.

- Before you conclude any customer interaction, ask

    "Is there anything more I can do for you?"
    "Are there any other questions that you would like me to answer?"

- When dealing with an upset or demanding customer, set appropriate limits if necessary. But get to the root causes of the frustration by actively and nondefensively listening. Empathize with the customer's perceptions, and whenever appropriate, apologize for the situation:

    1. "I know this is very frustrating, and I'm going to do everything I can to solve this problem for you."

2. "I'm sorry for the long wait. I'm here for you now, and I will spend as much time as necessary to address your concerns."

3. "I'm sorry that I don't have the authority to do what you're asking. Perhaps my supervisor can help you. I'll get her."

- Speak in a language the customer understands. Don't use buzzwords and industry-specific terminology or jargon.

- Utilize the following script when answering the telephone:

  1. "Good morning (afternoon or evening). This is (name of department and person). How may I help you?"

  2. Put a smile in your voice; don't appear rushed or bothered.

  3. If possible, answer the phone within three rings. It's everyone's job to ensure a timely response to department phone calls.

  4. Respond to callers and acknowledge walk-in customers appropriately. If you are talking to a walk-in customer and the phone rings, excuse yourself and answer the telephone. Ask the caller if he or she may be put on hold or called back. Return calls promptly.

Examples of Worst Customer Service Practices

- "It's not my job. I can't help you." "You're not my customer."

- "I will be right back" (and not return). "I'll be back in a minute" (and return a half-hour later).
- "I'm too busy. You'll have to find someone else."
- Sighing or eye rolling when asked to do something.
- Complaining to customers about other departments, co-workers or the company.
- Having personal conversations in front of or during interactions with the customer.
- Speaking a language that the customer doesn't understand.
- Talking down to customers in a condescending manner.
- Denying a customer's perceptions by saying "You're wrong" or "Don't be upset."

Specific Inspection Strategies

Once you have developed specific and behaviorally concise standards of conduct, you must constantly monitor and evaluate how effectively employees are adhering to performance expectations. In addition to customer service and employee satisfaction surveys, you can use three very effective inspection strategies:

- **MBWA (Management by Wandering Around).** Place yourself in a position to see and hear firsthand what's going on within your department. This will provide you an opportunity to immediately compliment or coach employees. It also offers you the opportunity to roll up your sleeves and get your hands dirty if the need exists, demonstrating that you are willing and able to do what you ask of your employees and that you're supportive in times of crisis.

• **Employee Rounding** is another very effective inspection strategy that increases your visibility and accessibility to staff. This also provides you the opportunity to utilize employees as internal consultants to advise you on the strengths of your department and on any specific needs for improvement. Your employees are closest to the work. They know what's working and what's not, who is performing as expected and who is letting the department down. Tap into this resource by touching base with your employees on a regular basis and asking them the following questions:

"What is working well today?"
"Should I be recognizing anyone for going above and beyond today?"
"Is there anything I can do for you while I'm here?"
"Are there any problems that I should know about?"
"I know you were sick yesterday. How are you feeling?"
"I'm about to talk with some of our customers about how they perceive the quality of our services. Is there anything I should know before I talk with them?"

By maintaining an ongoing dialogue with employees, you create the opportunity to recognize staff, identify problems and solicit solutions to help make their job easier, more satisfying and effective.

Customer Rounding. Demonstrate to employees that you make service quality a top priority by regularly meeting with and maintaining a direct relationship with your customers. Learn directly from customers how they feel about the quality of your services by asking the following questions:

"How are you today?"

"Our goal is to provide you with the very best service. How well are we doing at meeting this goal?"

"Is there anything more we can do to meet or exceed your expectations? What can we improve upon?"

"Is there anyone you would like me to praise? Can you tell me what they have done that has impressed you?"

"Are there any questions that I can answer?"

"Is there anything I can do for you before I leave?"

Be sure that you share customer feedback with employees, and follow up on all concerns that customers express. This activity will pay significant dividends in developing staff, improving customer satisfaction and demonstrating to employees your total commitment to service quality.

Every right implies a responsibility, every opportunity an obligation, every possession, a duty.

———————————————

John D. Rockefeller, Jr.

4

REASONS FOR POOR PERFORMANCE

There are six possible explanations for marginal performance. Your role as a manager is to accurately diagnose the root causes and administer appropriate remedies. Each cause is described below with accompanying strategies to facilitate positive change.

1. Inability to Do the Job

Employees cannot be successful if they don't possess the innate ability or aptitude (mental or physical) to perform the duties of their jobs (Chambers, 169). For example, working within the service industry is an emotionally intensive and physically exhausting activity. Success at serving customers requires a high degree of self-esteem and what Goleman (1998) refers to as *emotional intelligence*. Skill sets of successful employees include:

- **Self-control:** the ability to stay composed, remaining calm, confident and dependable during conflictual or difficult, pressure-filled situations. Employees who don't possess self-control are subject to mood swings and angry outbursts when things don't go as planned.

- **Conscientious behavior:** the willingness to take responsibility for one's mistake, correct the problem and take steps to ensure that it doesn't occur again. Employees who don't demonstrate conscientious behavior cover up, deny, alibi, minimize errors or scapegoat others.

- **Social skills:** the ability to demonstrate empathy, respect, tact and consideration. Employees who don't demonstrate strong social skills are judgmental, dogmatic, arrogant and manipulative.

- **Trustworthiness:** the integrity to do the right thing when no one is looking, keep one's promises, honor one's commitments and follow through on tasks until completion. Employees who don't demonstrate trustworthiness do half-hearted work, cut corners, do just enough to get by and leave work for others to complete.

- **High tolerance for diversity:** the ability to appreciate different points of view and work effectively with a variety of cultures, personalities, communication patterns and work styles. Employees who don't demonstrate a high tolerance for diversity alienate those people who don't look, think and act as they do.

As a manager you must know what is within your control to change and what is not. You can enhance a person's

WHAT YOU ACCEPT IS WHAT YOU TEACH

knowledge through education. You can develop a person's *skills* through training. It is questionable, however, whether emotional intelligence can be taught. What is also uncertain is the extent to which you can change the following traits:

- **Service ethic:** Can you really motivate someone to care? Either a person gets satisfaction out of doing something nice for someone or she doesn't.

- **Pride:** the fundamental belief that if it is a job worth doing, it's worth doing well; the recognition that your primary objective on the job is not to be *happy* — it is to be *successful*. Happiness is a byproduct of success. It comes from taking pride in one's work and seeing the positive results of one's efforts.

- **Attitude:** the willingness to cast a positive spin on events and remain optimistic and constructive when others around you are pessimistic, cynical and ready to give up.

- **Motivation:** the drive to excel and to continuously improve one's quality of performance. An employee's true motivation is *intrinsic*. Her desire to succeed is fueled by passion for the activity in which she is engaged. Her prevailing concern is to be the best she can be and to make a valuable contribution. Hard work or challenging situations are not regarded as a personal sacrifice because the employee genuinely wants to achieve outstanding results. Doing a good job is highly valued and has meaning in the employee's life.

- **Self-discipline:** the persistence, determination, and resilience to see things through to their satisfactory conclusion; deferring immediate gratification to attain long-term objectives.

Hire for Attitude, Train for Skill

View every position opening as a wonderful opportunity to select employees who have strong character and integrity. Even if you are interviewing a very experienced and technically competent candidate for employment, do *not* hire the person if he has a bad attitude, ineffective communication skills or a poor service ethic. You don't have the time or the skills to change his core personality. You are not his *psychologist*. You are his *manager*. He is who he is, and he is not likely to change that much.

On the other hand, consider hiring an inexperienced person who possesses positive personal attributes:

- He knows what he doesn't know and is willing to learn.

- He has the capacity to learn.

- He has strong emotional intelligence skills.

- You are willing and able to invest in him through a comprehensive new employee orientation process.

It is much easier to teach someone technical skills than it is to change a person's negative attitude or compensate for a lack of integrity, character or goodwill.

In summary, the best way to avoid performance problems is to not hire them in the first place. Use your probationary period wisely. Cut your losses early if you made a mistake in the interview process (you thought you were employing Dr. Jekyll, but you got Mr. Hyde). The employee is usually on his best behavior during the first six months. If he demonstrates a spotty attendance record, a negative attitude or dysfunctional conduct early on, it's much more likely to get worse than to improve.

2. Role Ambiguity

Before you can hold them accountable for outstanding outcomes, all of the employees on your work team must be clear about specific roles and the degree of independence they have to carry out their jobs. Role ambiguity almost always leads to interpersonal and intergroup conflict. Therefore, ensure that every employee has answers to the following questions:

- Do you know who is supposed to engage in what activities to accomplish our goals? What specifically is each person responsible for?

- Do you know how you are interdependent on other members of the team? Have you identified your expectations of others within and between job classifications, shifts, work units and departments? If you can't do your job unless others do theirs in a timely and effective manner, you must communicate your expectations and maintain an ongoing dialogue with them. Are you willing and able to confront one another when your needs are not being met?

- Are reporting relationships clear? Do you know who has the right to tell you what to do? Accountability must ultimately be focused on the individual level. Everyone must be held accountable to someone to achieve clearly defined results.

- Do you know how much independence and authority you have to make decisions, implement changes, allocate resources and spend time or money?

- Do you know what actions you can take independently without informing me before or after? When *must* you notify me to get permission to do something?

- Do you know what policies, procedures, guidelines and legal or regulatory mandates must be respected as you carry out your responsibilities?

- Do you know what resources exist or don't exist to facilitate goal accomplishment? What are the system barriers that may serve as impediments to success? Which of these obstacles can we overcome through creative problem solving, and which obstacles are realities we must adjust to and accept?

Maintain Flexibility in Your Performance Management Strategy

To be an effective manager, you must tailor your leadership style to the specific needs of each person on the work team. There are two types of employees on the skill/maturity continuum. On the high end is the *self-managed* employee who is technically competent and intrinsically motivated. This person is a self-starter and can be counted on to do the right thing when no one is looking.

It would be inappropriate to micromanage the self-managed employee, hover over her and watch every move she makes. Provide this person her earned independence, authority and control to do her job. Place resources in this person's hands to facilitate her success, and then get out of her way. It doesn't matter *how* this employee achieves positive outcomes, providing she succeeds through ethical and legal means. Simply hold the person accountable for the *results*, not specifically how she achieves the results.

On the low end of the skill/maturity continuum is the *high-maintenance* employee who does as little as possible to get by. This person cuts corners and violates policies and procedures whenever she can. This is an employee who is generally satisfied with her own mediocre performance. This employee has not yet earned your trust. Therefore, you must monitor her more closely to ensure that she does the right things, the correct way, within the specified time frame.

In other words, you don't have to be absolutely consistent in the way you manage employees. Strive to be consistent in the administration of personnel policies and procedures, but *treating all employees exactly the same is both ineffective and unfair.* Ensure that each employee is both comfortable and capable of exercising her level of responsibility and authority. Then monitor and evaluate to ensure that each employee responsibly exercises her authority to achieve positive outcomes. Freedom without responsibility is a very dangerous thing. It leads to anarchy. Regardless of the management style you embrace, always remain goal focused, results oriented and values driven.

3. Lack of Training

Make certain that you provide every employee an opportunity to succeed by providing skills training and development, coaching and counseling. Regularly schedule in-service education programs on paid, productive work time, and conduct the sessions as often as necessary to secure maximum attendance. Hold employees accountable for attending the programs, and when they return, ask the following questions to ensure you get a return on your training investment:

- Did you enjoy the session? What did you particularly like about it? How can we improve upon it next time?

- What did you learn from the workshop?

- How are you going to apply the knowledge or demonstrate the skill? What are you going to do differently as a result of attending the session?

- How should I inspect improved performance and measure better results?

By monitoring and evaluating workshop outcomes, you demonstrate a real commitment to a learning culture where every employee is expected to continually improve the quality of his performance.

To determine if your department has embraced a learning culture that invests in employees and facilitates their success at meeting your expectations, answer the following questions:

- Do employees understand that it is their responsibility to continuously improve their skill sets and knowledge base?

- Are individual and department learning goals established with accompanying methods, timetables, monitoring and evaluation strategies?

- Are employees recognized for achieving specific learning objectives? Are there consequences for stagnation?

- Do you encourage appropriate risk taking, experimentation and innovation? Do employees take the initiative to explore, search, question and challenge current assumptions about how things should be done?

- Do employees keep up with the trends in their field? Do they strive to be cutting edge in their areas of expertise?

- Are they active members of a professional association? Do they attend continuing education programs and read periodicals that keep them apprised of best practices?

- Do you play the role of teacher and coach for new employees, or do you delegate this responsibility to someone who has the time, skills, desire, and authority to develop employees?

4. Lack of Confidence to Do the Job

The employee may not *believe* that he has the necessary skills or knowledge to perform the job. This may be an expression of his insecurity or low self-esteem (Chambers, 19). He might be self-critical to a fault or very judgmental of co-workers. He may:

- pick on or demean others to make himself feel better

- regularly reject others' ideas as stupid or impractical

- ridicule others at every opportunity

- blame others for his errors or mistakes in judgment

- refuse to assist others

- attribute others' mistakes to ignorance, dishonesty, insincerity or malice

Assuming that you have already provided sufficient training and development, you may be limited in what else you can do to facilitate the employee's success. Strategies to build confidence include:

- offering genuine encouragement
- providing appropriate positive feedback that is tied to real results
- depersonalizing errors
- assigning tasks that match the employee's strengths whenever possible
- encouraging appropriate risk taking
- setting limits on aggressive behavior
- suggesting personal coaching or counseling
- teaching co-workers how to assertively respond to demeaning comments and how to set limits on abusive behavior

Always maintain your high standards, but recognize that each person is at his own stage on the learning curve. Fine-tune your performance improvement action plans to match the unique needs of each employee.

5. System Problems

Your employees might identify real or imagined obstacles that are preventing them from achieving an acceptable performance level. Therefore, you have to help employees separate *problems* from *realities*. There is no problem so difficult that it cannot be solved. If it can't be solved, it is not a problem. It is a reality. There will always be frustrating realities in any work situation. Employees must learn to accept realities and work to solve the problems that come with them.

By definition, a *problem* is an obstacle to an employee's success that can be solved. It is an obstacle that is within someone's control to fix. A *reality*, on the other hand, is an obstacle that is outside your or your employee's control to overcome. Examples of realities may include budgetary constraints, space limitations, old equipment or your inability to add more staff. It's not that you don't care about these obstacles to employee success, or that you are not supportive of your employees when they complain about these things. You simply can't *do* anything about them. Therefore, once realities are explained to employees, expect that they:

- accept and effectively adapt to obstacles that can't be overcome

- stop griping and dumping about things that cannot be changed

- focus on the *positive* aspects of the working condition

- take complete responsibility for their own constructive attitude, conduct, positive work and service ethic

- work to become a part of the solution to problems they identify. The message should be:

  "If you can solve a problem on your own, fix it. It's better to ask for forgiveness than permission. If you can't independently solve the problem, participate in department meetings or volunteer to be on a committee or task force. If you're not part of the solution, you're part of the problem."

Remove any system barrier that *is* within your sphere of influence to positively impact. But if you can't remove the obstacle, assess whether your performance expectations are realistic. Again, you cannot hold employees accountable for those things that are outside their control.

6. Attitudes of Resistance or Refusal

If a marginal employee has the mental and physical capacity to succeed, has been provided adequate training, specific performance standards and evaluation criteria, understands his role and possesses the necessary resources to succeed, you must then assume that the employee is *choosing* not to effectively perform the job.

If this is the correct diagnosis, the employee's unwillingness is a job performance issue, and you must engage in the following managerial practices to facilitate positive behavior change:

- Establish clear, short-term goals for the employee that meet the **S.M.A.R.T.** criteria:

  Specific: "This is what you specifically must do differently to meet my expectations."

  Measurable: "These are the indicators of success, or how I will know that you are meeting my expectations."

  Achievable: "While this performance improvement goal might be a stretch for you, it is an attainable, reasonable expectation."

  Relevant: "This goal is consistent with the values of the department and organization. My expectation for improvement is job related and driven by business necessity."

  Timely: "Here's *when* I expect you to see improvement."

- Increase your monitoring of the employee. Remember, a person with a bad attitude is a *high-maintenance* employee who requires more of your attention. Increase mandatory reporting frequency by regularly scheduling face-to-face review sessions in which specific progress is communicated. Also, consider conducting quarterly performance appraisals instead of waiting a full year to evaluate progress.

- Make certain that the employee's errors or counterproductive behaviors are dealt with *immediately*. Your failure to take quick action communicates acceptance of the employee's conduct and allows the employee to make a habit of poor performance.

- Maintain these controls until the employee demonstrates performance improvement on a consistent basis. Gradually loosen the controls as positive change is indicated. The employee can *earn* a decrease in controls by successfully meeting your performance expectations.

- Standards must be enforced uniformly and consistently. Do not single out individual employees without reason. Everyone must be consistently held accountable to the same performance expectations.

- Attitude should be the *last* place to look as the cause of poor performance, not the first.

Do or do not, there is no try.

_____

Yoda

COMMANDMENTS OF CONFRONTATION

You have already tried to be understanding and supportive. Perhaps you have looked the other way. Out of frustration you may have yelled, stomped your feet or pounded the table. You may have even pleaded with the employee to improve his quality of performance. Nothing has worked.

It's not a question of *whether* you should confront the problem employee, but *how* you will address the performance deficiency. Listed below are fifteen commandments of confrontation (rules of engagement) that will not only facilitate positive behavioral change but also enable you to maintain a positive work relationship with the employee. Remember, you can be tough as nails and remain a decent human being.

1. **Confront the employee privately behind closed doors, away from the public arena.**

Open criticism is humiliating. When you attack someone publicly, you provide the person no opportunity to save face or maintain self-esteem. The person is likely to get defensive and plot revenge. Onlookers will also be embarrassed and will probably identify and sympathize with the employee. They might think it could happen to them next.

There exists only one occasion when it is appropriate to criticize someone in front of customers or co-workers: If you catch an employee in the process of doing something illegal, unsafe or unprofessional and you are in a position to stop the wrongdoing, then you must immediately intervene. You should then apologize later for the public rebuke.

2. **Keep your conversations confidential.** Talk directly to the person with whom you have the problem, and never criticize one employee to another. When you talk *about* someone, it will most likely get back to him in a distorted and editorialized version. Trust in the relationship may be irreparably broken. Therefore, *always be loyal to those not present.* Once you violate someone's confidence, you may not get a second chance to rehabilitate the relationship.

3. **The best feedback is timely feedback** provided you are cool, calm and collected when delivering the message. Therefore, confront the employee as soon as possible after the incident. If you wait too long, by the time you do confront the employee, the feedback is likely to be too general and ambiguous, not instructive or constructive. Or, due to intervening events, you may forget to confront the person at all, missing your window of opportunity for coach-

ing and counseling. Don't let your discomfort at confronting employees keep you from giving timely, constructive feedback.

4. **Level *with* the employee. Don't *level* the employee.** Package your ideas in a constructive and instructive manner. Regardless of provocation, don't yell, swear, interrupt, stomp the floor or pound the table to get your message across. If you allow the employee to control your *emotions*, you are allowing him to control *you*. Don't give him that kind of control over you. *Operate from quiet strength.* Stay calm and focused.

5. **Do not get personal or use negatively loaded words** that will naturally induce employee defensiveness. Avoid terms like *stupid*, *lazy*, *incompetent*, *unprofessional* and *disrespectful*. These terms are hopelessly general and ambiguous, not specific or behaviorally concise. They don't tell the employee what actions are problematic. Rather than tell an employee that she has a "bad attitude," for example, describe the *behavioral manifestations* of the bad attitude:

"When I asked you to do something just now, you rolled your eyes and made a deep sigh as if you were doing me a favor. This is, after all, part of your job."

6. **Be specific regarding what the person should do or say differently** to meet your expectations and the consequences for not doing so:

"When you are finished with your own work, unless it is your break time, I expect that you make offers of assistance to others in need of help without being asked. Instead, I saw you leave the work area without telling anyone where you went. The next time this happens, you will receive a written warning."

You're not the employee's psychologist. You're her manager. It is often difficult to understand the psychological dynamics or motivation underlying someone's actions. But you do have the right to legislate professional conduct that is conducive to a positive work environment. Always focus on the behaviors and their negative impact on the department.

7. **Once you have made the point, don't keep repeating it.** It would be ideal for the employee to agree with what you're saying and apologize for his mistake, but it's not critical for purposes of managing performance. What *is* imperative is that the employee *understands* your specific expectations for change and the consequences for not meeting them. Before terminating the session, ask the employee to summarize what he heard you say, and document the critical elements of the discussion.

8. **Address one issue at a time.** Don't "sandbag" the employee by collecting misdeeds that have occurred over a significant period of time and then, in one single conversation, overload the person with a long list of complaints. When you inundate an employee with a litany of performance deficiencies, the person simply can't focus on any one particular issue. The conversation is a blur. The employee feels overwhelmed and hopeless. Of course, when you are conducting an annual performance appraisal, it *is* necessary that you discuss all of the employee's strengths and developmental needs. But for day-to-day dialogue, focus on one specific incident at a

time. Also, there should never be any surprises or new issues raised on the annual performance appraisal. If the employee was doing something wrong six months ago, you should have talked to him about it at the time. He could have corrected the problem had he only known about it.

9. **Be prepared to listen to the employee's perspective** before drawing any firm conclusions. Even if you catch an employee "dead to rights" doing something wrong, you may want to consider opening the dialogue by inviting the employee to explain his actions:

- "Help me understand why you just did that."

- "Let's discuss what just happened."

- "Can you tell me what was behind your actions?"

Things may not be as they appear at first blush. The employee's feedback may cause you to pause and reconsider your initial judgment. First get all the facts. Then draw your conclusions.

10. **Anticipate and plan for an immediate negative response to your message,** particularly if the employee has a history of resistance, defensiveness or denial when given constructive feedback. The employee's defensive response (verbal or nonverbal) can serve as an example of the employee's negative attitude or unwillingness to change. You may need to state your observation directly:

"I am trying to discuss this issue with you, but what I observe is your refusal to talk, the absence of any direct eye contact with me and the folding of your arms. This indicates to me that you're either not listening, resisting my message or not buying into anything that I'm saying."

Ask the employee to summarize her understanding of the need for change. If indicated, set up another meeting. In preparation for this meeting, ask the employee to develop an action plan describing what she will do to satisfy your concerns.

11. **Don't apologize for the confrontation.** By doing so, you detract from the seriousness of your message. The apology may also indicate that you feel guilty or that you lack confidence. When an employee makes a serious mistake, you would be remiss if you *didn't* provide corrective feedback. Holding people accountable for their actions is an integral and necessary part of your job.

12. **Offer to place resources in the employee's hands to facilitate his success at meeting your objectives.** This may include individual coaching, formal training and development, books, CDs or tapes. If appropriate, recommend that the employee utilize the resources of an employee assistance program to discuss sensitive personal issues that may be contributing to his performance deficiencies.

13. **Don't feel compelled to compliment an employee every time you confront him about a problem.** The "sandwich" approach to criticism suggests that you should first compliment the employee, next confront him about a mistake and finally compliment him before you terminate the discussion. This is a disingenuous and manipulative concept. Compliments are sometimes offered

to soothe the manager's discomfort with confrontation. Deal with your own discomfort and confront the employee whenever appropriate. Recognize employees whenever they deserve it. However, when a mistake is made, level with the employee. Don't mix your messages.

14. **Address real obstacles to employee success.** It is critical that you actively listen to an employee's concerns if she identifies a system issue that is serving as an impediment to her success. The employee may blame a co-worker or claim that she is overworked or stressed out and is therefore not responsible for her conduct. Maintain your focus on how the employee chooses to react to job frustrations. Address the legitimate causes of employee negativity that are within your control. But an imperfect work environment does not justify unprofessional conduct. People have a right to their feelings, but they should be held accountable for constructive and collaborative behaviors regardless of circumstance.

15. **Follow up with the employee.** Schedule a follow-up meeting before concluding the discussion; then put yourself in a position to monitor and evaluate performance improvement. Recognize the person when positive change occurs, thereby reinforcing more of the same behavior. Be prepared to mete out negative consequences if the performance deficiency continues.

Control over an employee is an illusion. You can't *make* an employee do anything or *force* behavior change on him. All you can (and must) do is clearly communicate your ex-

COMMANDMENTS OF CONFRONTATION

pectations, make resources available to set the employee up for success, monitor and evaluate outcomes, and recognize success or mete out consequences for failure. Once an employee knows what is expected, either he has the will or the skill to perform as expected, or he doesn't. In the end, you never really manage employees, only their performance. They are managing themselves.

Finally, regardless of circumstances, never publicly blame or penalize the entire work unit for the negative behaviors of one or some of its members. Hold the *individual* accountable for her performance. Each employee is ultimately responsible for her own work and service ethic, intrinsic motivation, positive attitude and constructive behaviors.

He who thinketh he leadeth and hath no one following him is only taking a walk.

_____

Author Unknown

A STEP-BY-STEP
COUNSELING MODEL

As indicated in a previous chapter, there is no one correct communication or leadership style. Each situation is different and every manager has her own unique way of approaching difficult conversations. There are specific communication strategies, however, that can lower an employee's defensiveness and make him more open to your performance feedback.

Listed below are sample scripts that will maximize your chances for achieving an effective employee dialogue. Tailor these statements to ensure that they are consistent with your own personality and the unique needs of the employee or situation.

1. State your observation.

- "Here's what I perceive is happening."
- "This is what I just observed."

2. Listen to the employee's response.

- "Help me understand what happened."

- "Tell me your thoughts. I'd like to hear your perspective."

- "Please share with me your perception of what just occurred."

3. If appropriate, summarize both responses.

- "Let's summarize our perceptions."

- "Here's what I heard you say."

4. State the specific expectation.

- "Here's what needs to be done differently."

- "Next time I want you to start (do more) or stop (do less) to meet my expectations."

5. Seek feedback.

- "I want to be sure that I have communicated effectively. Would you please paraphrase your understanding of my expectations for change?"

- "Let me summarize the changes that need to occur and get confirmation that you understand my expectations."

6. Discuss implementation strategies.

- "How will the change be accomplished?"

- "Let's talk about the steps you're going to take."

- "Within a week, please share with me how you are going to meet this expectation."

7. Identify monitoring and evaluation techniques.

- "How will we know if positive change has occurred?"
- "Here's how I will know if the positive change has occurred."
- "Here's when we will meet again to discuss progress on this issue."

8. State the consequences if change does not occur.

- "The next time an incident like this occurs, the following disciplinary action will be taken."
- "If I receive another complaint from a customer that represents a similar pattern of behavior, I will meet with you to listen to your side of the story. But if the customer's feedback is credible, I will no longer be able to give you the benefit of the doubt. The next step in the disciplinary process will be...."
- "Should you demonstrate a positive response, we will continue to monitor your performance to ensure that it is incorporated into your daily routine."

9. Offer resources to facilitate the employee's success at meeting your expectations.

- "Is there anything I can do to help you improve?"

- "I'd like to offer you the following resources to facilitate your success: additional coaching, formal training or an employee assistance counselor. Are you willing to take advantage of any of these resources?"

10. **Summarize once again agreements and understandings.**

- "Do you understand my expectations and the potential consequences for not meeting these expectations?"

- "Please summarize what my expectations are to ensure that we have communicated effectively. Are we on the same page regarding what actions you need to take?"

11. **Document the discussion through anecdotal records or by issuing a formal disciplinary action. Include the following details:**

- the date and time of the incident

- the date and time the discussion occurred (if different from the incident)

- a thorough description of the alleged occurrence (Double-check the validity and accuracy of your documentation. The employee may challenge your facts. Will they hold up under review?)

- the employee's response to the allegation

- a thorough description of your verbalized expectations for change with established timeframes as a target for performance improvement

- verbalized consequences of failure to make the change
- resources offered to help employee make necessary changes

If appropriate, secure the employee's signature indicating that he understands your expectations and the consequences for not meeting them. If the employee refuses to sign the corrective action, explain that his signature is not to signify agreement. It is to signify that he has read the document and understands what is expected of him. Invite the employee to write up his side of the story and assure him that you will attach his version of the incident to the corrective action document. Indicate on the form "The employee chooses not to sign" with your signature. In certain circumstances you may want to consider having another manager or a human resource representative observe the employee's refusal to sign and ask that person to sign as a witness.

12. **Follow up to inspect if positive change has occurred.**

- Place yourself in a position to notice.
- Review relevant documents.
- Proactively solicit feedback from customers, peers and the employee to assess performance improvement.
- Set follow-up meetings with the employee and keep them.

13. **Provide positive feedback and recognition as the employee meets expectations.** According to behavior modification principles, behaviors that

are reinforced get repeated. If you don't recognize positive change, you run the risk of extinguishing it.

14. **If positive change does not occur, provide additional counseling and/or corrective action.** By not implementing consequences, you are giving tacit approval for wrongful behavior, and your discussion becomes meaningless.

15. **Maintain an open line of communication with your human resource representative.** Ensure that you are adhering to personnel policies and procedures. Also, keep your own manager apprised of your actions to ensure that you have her support throughout the performance improvement process.

Counseling or discipline is:

- an inherent part of your job
- an effective process to help identify, correct or bring consequences to deficient performance and disruptive behavior
- a process for complying with legal, ethical and professional requirements in the event an employee must be terminated
- a good-faith process to facilitate an employee's success

Consider these additional points when you are administering corrective action (Chambers, 222):

- Do not use counseling or discipline as a mechanism to punish or as a tool to bludgeon an employee into submission.

- Do not apply discipline casually, impulsively or in an emotionally reactive manner.

- Be committed to following through before you get started. You must be willing to potentially lose the employee if performance improvement is not indicated.

- Consequences must be applied in an evenhanded and consistent manner. Even the appearance of preferential treatment or favoritism can be as dangerous as the real thing.

- An employee's apology for wrongdoing may be genuine, but her acceptance of appropriate consequences and her demonstration of performance improvement are what really matters.

- You can't measure *try*. The employee may in fact intend to improve, but the only meaningful unit of evaluation is *behavior change*. You must be able to see, hear or verify improved results.

Great Managers Are Effective Disciplinarians

While the negative connotation of discipline is one of condemning judgment—disapproval, reprimand or forced compliance—the *positive* use of discipline has entirely different associations:

- from the old French word *desciple*: one who accepts and helps to spread the teachings of another
- one of the original followers

- training expected to produce character, moral or mental improvement
- self-control

Leadership is about attracting *voluntary followers.* Employees follow the leader not out of fear or intimidation, but because they respect her and identify with her vision and values. They view her as a role model for positive attitudes and behaviors and want to follow in her footsteps.

You should use your position power whenever necessary to enforce policies and procedures and to set limits on dysfunctional behavior, but ultimately your authority rests on your personal credibility. As a leader you are viewed by employees as a person of integrity who is honest, trustworthy and believable. You are perceived to be caring and supportive, primarily motivated to achieve win-win outcomes, as opposed to controlling or repressing.

In the last analysis, position, power, title, credentials or degrees don't add up to credibility. Leaders achieve positive results through others not because of anything they say or do. They succeed because of *who they are or how they are perceived to be.*

Examples of Specific and Behaviorally Concise Performance Feedback

Listed below are general and ambiguous managerial comments made during coaching sessions or documented in performance appraisals. The feedback doesn't describe specifically what the employee is doing wrong. Following each one of these statements is a more specific and behaviorally concise way to articulate your expectations.

1. General feedback:

"Your attendance is really spotty. Your co-workers cannot depend on you. There will be serious consequences if this doesn't improve."

Specific feedback:

"In the last 90 days, you have had four unscheduled, unexcused absences of two days or less. Three of these absences occurred before or after a weekend or scheduled day off. In addition, you have been tardy ten minutes or longer three times within the same time period. The next unscheduled, unexcused absence or tardiness in 90 days will result in a written warning. Continued failure to come to work as the schedule requires could result in further disciplinary action up to and including discharge."

2. General feedback:

"You are lazy. You lack initiative. You have a bad work ethic."

Specific feedback:

"When you're finished with your own work, unless it's your break time, I expect that you make offers of assistance to others who may need your help. Or you can always work on the learning objective that we established on last year's performance appraisal. Don't read a newspaper or get involved in lengthy personal telephone conversations on paid, productive work time. Also, don't leave the work unit without anyone knowing where you are going or when you are returning.

This is a verbal warning. You will receive a written warning the next time you do this."

3. General feedback:

"You're too negative. I want you to improve your attitude."

Specific feedback:

"You keep complaining about things that no one can do anything about. You complain before and after meetings, but rarely contribute your ideas during the meetings. When you have a conflict, you talk to everyone *but* the person with whom you have the problem. I expect that you utilize the established department problem-solving and conflict-management protocols to get closure on issues. I also expect that you offer suggestions for problems that you identify and accept or adjust to those job frustrations that nobody can do anything about. You have a right to your feelings and opinions, but when you are frustrated or upset, I expect that you communicate your concerns in a professional manner."

4. General feedback:

"Our employee lounge is a mess. Clean it up."

Specific feedback:

"It's not up to Housekeeping alone to keep our employee lounge clean. I expect that everyone pick up after themselves. Wash your own dishes and cups, pick up the trash around the wastepaper basket and place your own personal belongings in a secure area. The last person who uses the microwave has the responsibility to clean it up for the next person."

5. General feedback:

"You are rude toward customers. I want you to be more pleasant."

Specific feedback:

"According to our customer service standards, it is expected that you follow appropriate communications when dealing with customers. Based on recent feedback from patient rounds and customer interviews (cite specific examples), it is evident that you are not adhering to these standards. I received feedback that you talk negatively about the organization to customers, that you carry on private conversations in public and that you conflict with co-workers in earshot of customers. These behaviors are not acceptable. You will receive corrective action the next time it is confirmed that you engaged in any of these types of activities."

6. General feedback:

"You are being insubordinate."

Specific feedback:

"Just now when I asked you to fax some documents for me, you snapped the papers out of my hand and mumbled something under your breath on the way to the fax machine. When returning the documents, you literally tossed the copies onto my desk. I find these actions very disrespectful and insubordinate. I would like to understand what is behind this behavior." Issue a written warning for insubordinate actions.

7. General feedback:

"You are disrespectful to me."

Specific feedback:

"On three separate occasions within the last week, I have said 'Hello' to you while passing you in the hallway. Each time I received no response from you. In fact, in the last instance, you not only refused to acknowledge me, you rolled your eyes and made an audible sigh. On the first occasion, I gave you the benefit of the doubt that you didn't hear me, or that you were lost in thought. But you must have heard my greetings the second and third time. I am willing to sit down with you to discuss whatever it is that's bothering you. If there is something I did that's upsetting you, let's talk about it. But in the meantime, I expect that when I say 'Hello,' you will acknowledge my greeting."

8. General feedback:

"Your quality of work is slipping. It's not up to our standards for cleanliness and safety."

Specific feedback:

"I inspected the rooms you cleaned over the past two days and I found blood on one of the bed frames. All of the televisions were dusty on the top and sides. Three shower floors had stains from previous use. One IV was not clean. The floors were not swept in two rooms. One bed table had food on it."

Preparing for Employees' Defensiveness

This is a list of potential negative responses to a manager's attempts at facilitating positive behavioral change. To effectively manage an employee's performance, you must anticipate and plan for such responses. How would you reply to the following employee statements?

- "Why are you singling me out? I'm not the only one guilty of this. I don't see you talking to anyone else about it!"

- "I think this is so unfair. You just don't like me. You're prejudiced, and I think that you're out to get me."

- "This is a bunch of (expletive). I'm not going to take this (expletive). You're full of (expletive)." Employee pounds the desk, violates your personal space, slams doors/drawers or threatens you.

- "I am not going to listen to this." Employee begins to walk away.

- With tears flowing down her cheeks, the employee responds: "I'm so sorry. I'm just an idiot. I'm so stupid. Maybe I should quit."

- "I know what I did was wrong. But I'm going through some personal problems right now. Can't you be a little more supportive?"

- "I'm really, really trying. That's all you can ask of me."

- "Okay. I made a mistake. But you never tell me when I'm doing a good job. And I'm not the only one who says this. Furthermore, you never let us know what's going on or ask our opinion on anything."

- "That's just your perception. It doesn't make it true."

- "You're accusing me of something that I didn't do. You were not there to observe it. Who told you this?"

- "I'm just being punished for speaking up. This is a form of retaliation. I'm just not going to say anything anymore."

- "Nobody knows this job better than I do. No one works harder than I do. That's what really matters. If co-workers have an issue with my behavior, that's their problem."

- "I know this is a problem but it's not my fault. I can't do my job until someone else completes his work."

- "What do you expect me to do when a customer is going off on me? Turn the other cheek? Be sensitive and understanding when he's verbally abusive? When customers are nice to me, I'm nice back. They get what they give!"

- "You say the customer is always right. But sometimes customers are wrong. They have unrealistic expectations and make demands on me that I can't possibly meet. What do I do then?"

- "You can't expect me to smile all the time. I'm a human being too. I'm entitled once in a while to have a bad day or to be in a foul mood. You should be sensitive to my psychosocial needs."

- "This is all well and good, but who has the time for practicing outstanding customer service? We're already short-staffed, overworked and stressed out. Management keeps cutting back on resources and making changes that hamper our ability to maintain quality. Nobody cares about us. And they still expect us to be nice. Give me a break!"

- "This workshop/meeting to improve service quality was OK. But nothing's going to change. It's a waste of time!"

Utilizing Anecdotal Records

As discussed in this chapter, there should never be any surprises or new issues raised on a year-end appraisal if you have been providing feedback to employees on a regular basis. Performance evaluation is an everyday process. Consider using an anecdotal record form (page 86) that documents your conversations with employees relative to critical incidents that occur throughout the year. This record will help you support your ratings of employees during the year-end performance appraisal.

If the occurrence that you are noting is a positive one, document the form of recognition that you provided. If it is a negative occurrence, document the employee's response to the allegation of wrongdoing. Does the employee, for example, acknowledge or deny the allegation? What is the employee's explanation of the negative result? Does the employee recognize the magnitude of the mistake and understand what he needs to do differently next time? Does the employee commit to positive change?

Also document what specific corrective action steps you are taking in response to the negative occurrence. Are you providing coaching and counseling or other resources to help the employee make needed changes? Is a verbal warning being issued indicating that the next negative occurrence will result in formal disciplinary action? What is your plan for follow-up?

Sample Anecdotal Record Form

Employee: _____

Job Title: _____

Date: _____

Description of occurrence (positive or negative):

_____

_____

_____

If positive occurrence, form of recognition provided:

_____

_____

_____

If negative occurrence, document employee's response to allegation. What is employee's explanation of event? Does employee acknowledge wrong doing, apologize, commit to positive change?

_____

_____

_____

Document coaching/counseling, other resources provided. If verbal warning is issued, document the stated consequences.

_____

_____

_____

Checklist for Discipline

		Yes	No
1.	The employee's actions are in violation of organization or department written policy, procedure, guideline or protocol.	☐	☐
2.	The requirement is based upon business necessity: the efficient and orderly operation of the organization depends upon this requirement. It is job related, based on the nature, function and scope of the job.	☐	☐
3.	The employee had advanced knowledge of the requirement and the consequences for not meeting it.	☐	☐
4.	The requirement does not put the employee at risk legally, ethically or professionally. It is also not unsafe for the employee, co-workers or customers.	☐	☐
5.	The employee has been treated the same way others have been treated under similar circumstances. There is consistency in the administration of corrective action without regard to race, color, national origin, religion, sex or sexual orientation. Reasonable accommodations have been made for any job-related disability.	☐	☐

Yes   No

6. An investigation has been conducted in a ☐   ☐
thorough, fair and objective manner. All
facts were considered including the context
in which the violation took place.

7. The investigation produced sufficient evi- ☐   ☐
dence of the employee's wrongdoing.

8. The severity of the corrective action fits ☐   ☐
the violation. The magnitude of the violation is sufficient grounds for punitive action, or there is a pattern of employee conduct that warrants this discipline. You have
considered the extent of harm done (or
potential harm done) to the organization's
reputation or state of customer/employee
relations.

9. There is a reasonable time frame between ☐   ☐
the violation and the administration of disciplinary action.

10. You have provided written documentation ☐   ☐
that effectively explains the rationale for
corrective action. An independent, objective person who reads the document would
deem the consequences reasonable and fair.

Performance Management Planning Worksheet

What are you doing to facilitate performance improvement in those employees who are deficient in their technical competence, customer service or teamwork skills? Consider developing a performance improvement action plan that documents:

- the employee's strengths to build upon
- the employee's specific needs for improvement
- monitoring, evaluation and follow-up strategies to be utilized for measuring success
- consequences of failure to positively change
- available resources to help the employee succeed
- timetables to assess and communicate progress

Likewise, what are you doing to recognize and reward your best employees? How can you specifically word your praise so that it is clear, effective and meaningful to the employee? Will the praise be public, private or both? Will it be oral or written? If written, how will the record be kept? If the recognition is in the form of promoting or delegating additional responsibilities, how can you be sure that it is welcomed and not aversive to the employee?

Consider utilizing the Performance Management Planning Worksheet on page 90 to track and document the employee's performance relative to three key results areas: technical competence, customer service and teamwork.

Performance Management Planning Worksheet

Rate each employee on a continuum of 1 (Excellent) to 5 (Minimum Acceptable) and develop your action plan to recognize achievement and hold employees accountable for performance improvement.

Employee	Technical Competence	Customer Service	Teamwork	Action Plan to Recognize and/or Facilitate Positive Change
	1 2 3 4 5	1 2 3 4 5	1 2 3 4 5	
	1 2 3 4 5	1 2 3 4 5	1 2 3 4 5	
	1 2 3 4 5	1 2 3 4 5	1 2 3 4 5	
	1 2 3 4 5	1 2 3 4 5	1 2 3 4 5	
	1 2 3 4 5	1 2 3 4 5	1 2 3 4 5	
	1 2 3 4 5	1 2 3 4 5	1 2 3 4 5	
	1 2 3 4 5	1 2 3 4 5	1 2 3 4 5	
	1 2 3 4 5	1 2 3 4 5	1 2 3 4 5	
	1 2 3 4 5	1 2 3 4 5	1 2 3 4 5	
	1 2 3 4 5	1 2 3 4 5	1 2 3 4 5	

Absent Consequences,
You're Merely Offering a Suggestion.

Author Unknown

7

MANAGING THE PASSIVE-AGGRESSIVE EMPLOYEE

Passive-aggressive employees present one of the most difficult performance-management challenges any manager will ever address. Passive-aggressive employees will go out of their way to avoid you. When you ask them a question, they are short and snippy. When they have complaints, they won't talk *to* you about what is bothering them. They will talk *about* you and try to rally others against you. They incessantly gripe and dump, moan and groan, sulk and pout. But they refuse to engage in constructive dialogue with you to solve the problem. If you call a departmental meeting to discuss the issue, they will not attend. If they do happen to attend, they will not participate. As soon as the formal meeting ends, however, the *informal* meeting begins:

"This is *so* unfair."

"Nobody *ever* listens to us."

"It doesn't do any good to say what's on your mind. It won't change anything, so what's the point?"

"This will *never* work."

"This is a bad idea. Sounds stupid. No way."

"Management doesn't know what it's doing or doesn't seem to care. They're *never* supportive."

Passive-aggressive employees may also communicate to you that they are unhappy through gestures that are not very subtle in nature. You will observe:

- eye rolling or arm crossing

- frowning or lack of eye contact

- sneers, smirks or sighs

But while they communicate their discontent through this nonverbal language, they refuse to tell you specifically what they're unhappy about. You should be able to read their mind. And, if you ask them to tell you what's wrong, their response will likely be:

"Nothing."

"You should know."

"Isn't it obvious?"

"It won't do any good to talk about it."

"It doesn't matter."

Passive-aggressive employees often feel that they are being treated unfairly, and they blame *you* for their own negative attitude. In fact, they expend a great deal of time and energy complaining about you and the working conditions. They can't let go of previous events, and they keep negative emotions alive. They may repeatedly tell the same old story about how you or another employee took advantage of them. They feel captive and victimized by their circumstances, and they cite their sense of powerlessness as a reason for not taking positive action.

Passive-aggressive employees personalize conflicts and demonize those with whom they disagree. Their initial response to conflict is anger, resentment or the need for revenge. They are generally mistrustful of people. They look for hidden agendas and ulterior motives.

They don't actively listen when you try to give them constructive feedback, and they easily get defensive when you confront them about a mistake. Their first impulse is to:

- deny
- cover up
- alibi (co-workers, the system)
- scapegoat
- minimize the importance of the error

Passive-aggressive employees thrive on gossip and rumors. They don't want to be miserable alone, so they like to remind others why they too should be angry. They resent others who *do* enjoy their jobs, and they question the motives of anyone who gets along with management. They may be *negative opinion leaders*: Co-workers use them as a sounding board to complain and agitate.

They come to work with a chip on their shoulder. They act like they're doing you a favor reporting for duty. They are resistant to change and opposing beyond reason. Their irritability is incessant and debilitating to everyone in the department. They cooperate only with co-workers that they personally like or who have "earned" their respect.

Many passive-aggressive employees frequently demonstrate a prima donna attitude. They are self-absorbed, narcissistic individuals who care only about themselves, their own shift or work unit (Chambers, 93):

"Because I want it, I deserve it and I should have it."

"What is fair is whatever works best for me."

"What is best is whatever action serves my immediate self-interest."

"What is right is however I define it."

To make matters worse, passive-aggressive individuals believe that there is nothing wrong with their behavior, that their actions or attitudes are justifiable given their situation and that management's response to their negativity is always unfair and personal. When you confront them, their initial response is likely to be:

"You don't like me."

"You're just out to get me."

"Why are you singling me out?"

"Don't do this to me. It is so unfair."

"This must be in retaliation for speaking out."

"My technical skills are the only things that matter. Nobody knows this job better than I do. So what's the problem?"

The *problem* is that all it takes is one person who demonstrates these characteristics to adversely impact the culture of your department. It is so much easier to tear down than to build up. One negative, mean-spirited person, if not stopped, can raise havoc with group morale and productivity.

Specific Strategies for Managing the Passive-Aggressive Employee

Teach Employees Assertive Fair-Fighting Techniques

Children do not necessarily learn effective communication and conflict resolution skills in the home. Respect for peers and authority is not always evident in the public schools. Therefore, by the time little Tim and Jane grow up and enter your organization, they may not know how to manage disagreements, respond to constructive criticism or respectfully ask for what they want. By default, it becomes your responsibility to teach employees effective listening, conflict management and problem-solving skills.

Conflict is not bad or good. Conflict just *is*. It is a natural and inherent part of work. How employees *deal* with conflict can be good or bad, constructive or destructive. Do your employees demonstrate goodwill or malice toward co-workers when problems arise? Do they avoid conflict and therefore not address important issues? Do they attend to only what is in their own individual and immediate self-interest, or do they consider what is best for the team in the long run?

Assertiveness is the best strategy for managing conflict and solving problems because it is a collaborative approach geared toward a win-win outcome. When someone is assertive, she depersonalizes the conflict. She channels her energies toward solving the problem, rather than defeating the other person. She also makes a real attempt to understand the feelings of the other person as opposed to judging the other person.

When someone is assertive, using "I" statements, she simply describes the problem from her own point of view and the negative impact that problem is having on her. She communicates the problem without attacking the person, and she remains constructive, regardless of how the other person behaves.

Listed below are fifteen specific assertive fair-fighting strategies that will increase employees' chances for effectively managing on-the-job conflicts. Please note that many of these techniques are similar to the commandments of employee confrontation presented in Chapter 5. Teach these rules of engagement and hold all employees accountable for them.

Fair-Fighting Techniques

1. **Don't expect perfection.** Maximize people's strengths, minimize their weaknesses and adjust to their imperfections. If you expect perfection in others, you are destined to lead a life of self-righteous indignation. If you expect perfection in *yourself*, you are destined to lead a life of guilt and frustration. You won't be able to live up to your own expectations.

2. **Choose your fights with discretion.** Some problems just aren't worth complaining about. If you gripe about every little thing, you will gain the reputation of being a complainer or agitator. Furthermore, nobody will take you seriously when a *real* problem does require attention. The most credible employees are those individuals who don't often complain. However, when they raise an issue of concern, people listen because they have earned the

WHAT YOU ACCEPT IS WHAT YOU TEACH

right to be heard. Don't go to the mat on everything. Know the hills you are willing to die on, but there should be few of them. Don't sweat the small stuff. (And it's almost always small stuff.)

3. **Talk directly to the person with whom you are having the problem.** Understand that when you talk negatively about people, it *will* get back to them, only in a distorted fashion. Their feelings will be hurt. Communication breaks down. Managing conflicts by talking directly, honestly, and respectfully to others takes courage. But if you don't ask for what you want, you may never get it, and not taking this risk may be the greater risk. After all, people can't read your mind.

4. **Talk to the person behind closed doors** within the spirit of confidentiality and non-competitiveness. Don't criticize anyone in public. It only leads to embarrassment, and it provokes the person's defensiveness. You provide the person little opportunity to save face and maintain self-esteem. He may plot revenge.

5. **Be cool, calm and collected** when you confront the person. Be centered by taking the time to figure out what you are thinking and feeling. Don't lead with your emotions. Avoid yelling, swearing, interrupting, pounding the table or stomping your feet. Don't call people names. Be mindful of the effect that your message (both verbal and nonverbal) will have on the other person. If you are so angry that you don't trust what you're going to say next, don't say anything at all. Take a timeout. Less is more. Words said in anger can sting the soul. They can leave emotional scars that last long

after physical wounds are healed. Your feedback should make it easier, not harder, for the person to change in the desired direction.

6. **Be issue oriented, not personality oriented.** Level *with* the person, don't *level* the person. Simply describe the person's behavior (without attacking him) and the negative impact this behavior has on you. Then describe what the person could do differently to meet your expectations.

7. **Be open to different interpretations of the same event.** You don't have a corner on the truth. You only have your *perceptions* of reality. Simply share your point of view with the person and ask for his perspective.

8. **Don't sandbag or collect misdeeds**, building up personal resentment for the person in the process. Deal with one issue at a time as it arises. The best feedback is timely feedback. Therefore, speak to the person as soon as possible after the event occurs, providing that you have control over your emotions.

9. **The truth does not always set you free, and brutal honesty is not always a virtue.** It would be a dangerous world if we all said what was on our mind at the time we were thinking it to the person we were thinking it about. Don't say anything to the person that you will regret later. Don't unleash your severest blow. Once you say something in anger, you cannot take it back. The person may forgive you, but she may never forget what you said. And she may always wonder if that is what you really feel: Did the truth really come out in a fit of anger?

10. **Give everyone you deal with an opportunity to save face.** This is particularly important when it is obvious that the person made a mistake. You know it and the person knows it. Give the person room to maneuver by providing him the opportunity to admit wrongdoing. Don't rub his nose in it. And avoid reminding him that "I told you so."

11. **Know when to terminate the discussion.** If, in the course of a confrontation, you have repeated your best arguments more than once, it is likely that you are beating a dead horse or going around in circles. Agree to disagree for the time being, and come back to the discussion later if necessary.

12. **Get a third-party resource** whenever appropriate to be a sounding board or to help mediate the conflict. Sometimes you need to talk with someone who has the psychological distance and objectivity necessary to give you advice on how to best handle the conflict. This person may be your manager or a human resource professional. Choose someone whose advice you value, but who will not necessarily tell you what you want to hear.

13. **Put the conflict behind you and start a new day.** Not all work conflicts can be resolved, but they must be effectively managed. Don't get stuck in a conflict mode. There will always be conflict in a close work relationship, but in between the conflicts, try to reaffirm the positive aspects of working together.

14. **Good professional relationships do not mean you have to be friends.** So don't use personal dislikes as an excuse for a breakdown in com-

munication. You don't need to like someone on a personal basis to work effectively with her. Certainly it is easier to work with someone you like, but it is not a precondition for a successful working relationship. You can be friendly with someone without being friends. You can say "hello" to her in the morning, "goodbye" in the afternoon, offer her help and expect her to offer you help. Just be civil and exhibit a professional demeanor for the time you do have to work together. Regardless of your feelings toward the person, effective communication and cooperation are necessary to achieve department objectives.

15. **Don't violate any of the above fair-fighting principles** even when the other person chooses to ignore them. Control over others is an illusion. You are not responsible for what others say or do, but you are *always* responsible for your own behavior regardless of provocation.

Create a Department Protocol for Conflict Management

Develop a structured process for employees to solve problems with one another so that you don't always have to get in the middle of every interpersonal conflict. You are their manager, not their parent. Your employees are not siblings who are competing for your approval. Therefore, share the following conflict management protocol with employees and hold them accountable for adhering to it:

1. **Speak up.** Find your sense of entitlement to stand up and support yourself. No matter who you are, no matter your title or status, you deserve to be treated

with dignity and respect. Your feelings are legitimate and valuable.

2. **Establish a goal for the interaction.** Determine in advance what you want to accomplish when the discussion is completed:

   - "What exactly do I want or need?"
   - "How is this expectation not being met?"
   - "Is my expectation reasonable?"
   - "What do I want the person to start (do more of) or stop (do less of) to satisfy my need?"

3. **Empathize with the person.** Demonstrate an appreciation that the person's perceptions, right or wrong, are real and legitimate to him. A person's perceptions *are* his reality. Anticipate the person's potential for defensiveness, anger, resentment, confusion or feelings of being treated unfairly. Also anticipate the possibility that the person might cry, sulk, withdraw or shout. How will you respond? Be prepared to handle any of these possibilities.

4. **Don't make assumptions about the person's intentions.** You don't always *know* what the other person is thinking. His intentions are invisible to you. They exist only in the person's heart and mind. And, no matter how real your assumptions are about the person's intentions, they are often incomplete or just plain wrong.

5. **Intervene early.** Try to solve the problem at the earliest and most informal levels by talking directly to the co-worker *before* you get your manager involved.

6. **Package your message in a constructive manner.** Don't use judgmental terms that will induce defensiveness:

- "You are being inconsiderate."

- "You are being lazy."

- "You are so rude!"

A more effective way to begin the conversation is

- "Help me understand why you did that."

- "My perception is...."

- "What you did (describe behavior) had this effect on me: I thought/felt/needed...."

7. **Don't accuse the person of having bad intentions.** Accusing her of trying to hurt, upset or ignore you will naturally make her defensive. More important, you can't *prove* whether this was her motive. It is an unsubstantial claim that you can't defend.

8. **Involve someone else when needed.** If you anticipate denial or defensiveness, or if you are afraid of making the situation worse, consider utilizing a third-party resource for assistance in managing the conflict. But don't go to just anyone for assistance. Ensure that the person with whom you seek counsel meets the following criteria:

- The person has good listening skills.

- The person is objective. She has no personal self-interest in the outcome of the conflict.

- The person has credibility. You trust this person to give sound advice. The person has common sense.

- The person will maintain your confidentiality.

- The person is prepared to tell you what you don't necessarily want to hear. The person may empathize with what you are going through, but she may not necessarily agree with how you are handling the situation.

Make certain that you clarify your expectations of the selected third-party resource: Are you using this person as a sounding board? If so, you want the person to understand what happened but do nothing with the information. Do you want the person to offer you advice on how to handle the situation? If yes, ask her to coach you on what to say or even role-play a conversation with your co-worker. Do you want the person to intervene in your behalf, such as bringing both parties together to facilitate a dialogue? But, don't expect the third-party resource to do your talking for you. That's your job.

When You Are Confronted

1. **Listen to what the person has to say.** Don't automatically act defensively:

- "You are wrong."

- "Yes, but...."

- "That's *not* what happened!"
- "Who are you to tell me what to do? You're not my boss. I don't have to listen to you!"

2. **Seek to understand before you seek to be understood.** When someone is upset, his fundamental need is to be understood, not agreed with. And when the person is not listening to you, it's not always because he is stubborn. It may be because he doesn't feel heard or he senses that his feelings are not being validated. Therefore, the best way to lower someone's anxiety is to actively listen and ask open-ended, nonjudgmental questions that demonstrate genuine curiosity:

- "Can you say a little more about how you see this?"
- "How do you see this situation differently?"
- "What impact have my actions had on you?"

3. **Empathize and apologize whenever appropriate:**

- "I'm sorry that you're so upset. This wasn't my intent."
- "I can see this is really hard for you. Thank you for sharing it with me."
- "I am trying to understand this better. Can you tell me again what is it that I said or did that made you so angry?"
- "Can you give me an example of what you're saying I do?"

- "What is it exactly that you would like me to do next time so as to avoid upsetting you?"

4. Verify your understanding by summarizing what you heard the person say:

- "What I hear you telling me is...."
- "Let me summarize what you're asking of me."
- If the responses you get are not entirely clear, keep digging:
- "I'm still unclear about something."
- "What I'm still confused about is...."

5. Describe the situation from your point of view:

- "My perspective on the event is different. I would like to share with you how I see it and get your response."
- "Let me share with you my perception of what happened."

6. Be prepared to negotiate:

- "Here's what I'm willing to do. Is this acceptable?"
- "Here's what I need from you. Is that okay?"
- "What do you need from me to make it easier to do what I'm asking?"
- "I can do what you're asking of me, but I first need this from you."

7. **If necessary, agree to disagree.** Discuss with the co-worker where you go from here. Not all conflicts can be resolved, but they need to be effectively *managed* or customer service and team morale suffer.

Managing conflict is almost never about getting the facts. It is about different perceptions, judgments and values. It is about what a particular situation means to the co-workers involved. Effective conflict resolution requires assertive communication, active listening, problem solving, achieving closure and moving on (Stone, Patton, Heen and Fisher, 10).

Final thoughts on managing the passive-aggressive personality:

1. Remember to focus on the employee's behaviors, not her personality (Topchik, 84). You don't have the time or skill to change the employee's core personality, but you can and must address unacceptable behaviors.

2. Describe in specific terms the negative behaviors and their impact. If there is no effect on performance, morale, customers, productivity or quality, then you have no sound basis to intervene.

3. When confronting the passive-aggressive employee, he may immediately respond in a defensive manner. Use this "here and now" behavior as an example of his being closed to constructive performance feedback and immediately set limits on abusive conduct.

4. Be open to the employee's feedback. There may be a legitimate reason for his negativity, and perhaps you can do something about it.

5. Identify alternative constructive behaviors that the employee is expected to demonstrate even if there is a legitimate system issue to be addressed.

6. Articulate the consequences of failure to be a constructive and collaborative team player.

7. Utilize department-specific standards of conduct for teamwork as the criteria by which the employee will be judged.

8. Monitor and evaluate the employee's progress and provide feedback. If the behavior improves, recognize it. It if doesn't, follow the organization's corrective action procedure.

When a manager compromises a principle one time,
the next compromise is right around the corner.

———————————————

Zig Ziglar

MANAGING THE
INSUBORDINATE EMPLOYEE

The insubordinate employee does not legitimize, sanction or submit to your authority as his manager. His insubordination is a testing of boundaries or limits. If the employee perceives a weakness in you, he may initiate a challenge just to see how far he can go until you push back (Chambers, 192). If you fear the employee's reaction to reasonable requests, the employee will sense this, and you may experience *unending terror.*

Insubordination is most common when a manager is new to the position and her mettle has not yet been tested, is promoted from within the work unit and is now supervising her former peers, or is younger in age than the employees she manages. Insubordination is also common when the organizational culture does not support unpopular, yet necessary, management decisions or when employees believe a corrective action is unfair and arbitrary. When these con-

ditions occur, some employees may feel a need to demonstrate their bravado by outright defiance and "in your face"
conduct.

Examples of an employee's insubordinate behavior
include:

- directly refusing (without an acceptable explanation) to
  do what you ask of him

- yelling or swearing when you try to carry on a
  discussion

- turning his back and walking out on you, unilaterally
  disengaging from a discussion, or telling you he
  doesn't have time to discuss this with you right now

- making demeaning statements, such as "You're being
  ridiculous," "That's stupid" or "You're crazy"

- constantly interrupting or cutting you off

- making threatening remarks such as "I know where you
  live," "You better watch your back" or "I'd be careful if I
  were you"

- clenching a fist, violating your personal space, flipping
  you the finger or exhibiting other derogatory, demeaning
  nonverbal behaviors

Following one of these episodes, the employee may
apologize, feigning regret, but then repeat the same offense.
The cycle continues. Or the employee may say that he is
sorry but then rationalize his actions:

"You provoked me."

"You're too sensitive." "You're overreacting." "You're taking
this personally."

"I didn't mean to offend you." (He wants to be judged by his intent rather than by the effect of his behavior.)

"I was stressed out." "I was having a bad day."

"This is just the way I am. Deal with it."

"Okay, I was wrong. But this doesn't justify a corrective action." (He is unwilling to be held accountable and to face the consequences of his behavioral choices.)

Specific Strategies for Managing the Aggressive Employee

If you accept abuse from someone, you are teaching him to give you more abuse. What you accept is what you condone. You have a *responsibility* to set limits with insubordinate or aggressive employees. Indeed, appropriate limit setting is the only response this type of employee understands. But be careful. If you let your guard down, an aggressive employee can provoke you into saying something that you will later regret. When the employee is trying to drag you in the mud with his dysfunctional behavior, don't join him. Maintain the high ground. Operate from quiet strength by responding in a calm, yet firm manner:

1. Immediately set limits and gain control over the interaction:

   "There is no reason to shout. Please lower your voice. We need to have this discussion in a calm and collected manner."

   "You may not swear at me."

   "Please do not interrupt me. I listened to what you had to say. Now it's my turn to speak."

"Please remain in the room until we're finished with this discussion."

2. Communicate your expectations regarding the acceptable format for addressing an issue:

   "You and I can disagree, but we will discuss this issue in a respectful, calm manner."

3. Whenever times permits, allow the employee to state his objections. If, after listening to the employee's response, you conclude that your directive is still valid, provide a clear warning of consequences for continued noncompliance:

   "You are refusing to do what is expected without a satisfactory explanation. I am going to ask you one more time. If you refuse again, you will be immediately suspended with the possibility of discharge pending further investigation. Knowing what the consequences will be, what is your choice?"

   "Under no circumstances will this disrespectful behavior be tolerated. If you swear one more time, the consequence will be an immediate suspension or discharge. Will you stop using inappropriate language, or do I have to send you home?"

4. If the direct refusal or disruptive behavior continues, implement corrective action immediately and document the incident. Factually summarize:

   • the date and time of the occurrence

   • a thorough description of the incident including what you requested, the employee's response and your verbal warning of consequences

   • the specific corrective action taken

Notes:

If I am not for myself, then who will be for me?

And, if I am only for myself, then what am I?

And if not now, when?

———————————————

Hillel, the Elder

MANAGING MARTYRS

Employees must understand that there are no victims, only volunteers. If they are unwilling to stand up for themselves or lack the courage of their convictions, then it is absurd to expect you to take their issues seriously.

Martyrs avoid confrontation at all costs. They say "Yes" when they want to say "No." They volunteer for labor-intensive and time-consuming tasks without thinking things through. As a result, they frequently over commit. They become resentful of those individuals they are helping and get frustrated with themselves for taking on more than they can handle.

Employees who play this role will do anything you ask of them and more. They even volunteer to do jobs that others won't or can't do, compensating for co-workers' shortcomings. At the same time, they complain to significant others about their workload and co-workers who don't do their fair share.

Demonstrating acute passivity, these employees:

- walk away from upsetting situations rather than face them directly

- apologize even when they have done nothing wrong just to avoid a conflict

- feel guilty or automatically responsible when someone disapproves of their actions

- ask permission to do things when they already have the authority to act

- allow themselves to be repeatedly interrupted

- precede their remarks with disqualifying phases such as

  "This is only my perception."

  "I may be wrong about this."

  "This may sound stupid."

They also display nonverbal signals that are interpreted by others as weak, vulnerable or self-deprecating such as avoiding eye contact, looking down or to the side when spoken to, appearing afraid, stunned or about to cry.

Because they are conflict-aversive, martyrs allow themselves to be willing victims of a co-worker's aggressive or passive-aggressive behavior. Instead of speaking up for themselves and taking a stand, they make rationalizations for their self-imposed impotence:

- "The situation is not that bad. I can live with it."

- "It won't do any good talking to the person. Nothing will change. So what's the point?"

- "I don't know *how* to confront the person. I might say things that I later regret."

- "I might lose my temper or cry."

- "I might hurt the person's feelings."

- "The person might not like me."

- "It could make the situation worse. I could open up a can of worms. We might not talk to each other after this."

- "The person might plot revenge. I've been burned before. I refuse to be burned again. It's not worth taking the risk."

- "I don't have the right to speak up. I might be overstepping my bounds."

As a result, martyrs typically defer to others at the expense of their own needs, and they allow themselves to be taken advantage of. This may lead to depression, withdrawal (escape activities), pent-up anger, displacement of frustrations onto others who are willing to be scapegoats (often family members) and physical symptoms such as headaches or ulcers.

Strategies for Dealing With Martyrs

Everyone deserves to be treated with dignity and respect. If someone feels that she is being treated poorly, she must learn how to ask for what she wants and demand to be heard and understood. To facilitate this process:

- Coach employees on how to ask for help or confront a co-worker who is not doing his fair share.

- Ensure that every employee is held accountable to quality and productivity standards.

MANAGING MARTYRS

- Don't pile more work on those employees who are willing and able to perform, while substandard employees are given a pass.

- Provide the real contributors the recognition they deserve.

- Remind your productive employees that they can't do everything themselves. Expect them to start standing up for themselves and setting limits on co-workers who demonstrate lazy or abusive behaviors.

All employees must know that they have an *obligation* to confront someone whose behavior negatively impacts the quality of performance or reputation of the department:

> When we witness an injustice, we have a duty to argue. When we see human beings unjustly used, disrespected, exploited, injured, we have a duty to argue. When we hear unjust statements, we have a duty to not permit the poison to spread unabated....
>
> We have a duty to argue at home. We have a duty to argue with those we love, with our mates and our children. We have a duty to argue for ourselves and with ourselves. Yes, we even have a duty to argue with God. Having provided us the skill, I take it that God would be greatly disappointed should it go untested. (Spence, 16-17)

All that is necessary for the existence of wrongdoing within your organization is that good people do nothing. Problems will never get corrected if employees act as if they see no evil, hear no evil, refuse to speak up or remain afraid to get involved when wrongdoing occurs.

120

Sometimes you just have to create
what you want to be a part of.

———————————————

Geri Weitzman

10

MANAGING GOSSIP
AND THE FEAR OF CHANGE

The best antidote for rumors and gossip is to give employees the information and facts they need to make informed decisions. Help employees separate fact from fiction. Be accessible for answering questions. On a regular basis, ask employees "What's the rumor of the day?" This gives you the opportunity to confirm, deny or investigate "the word on the street."

You can never completely eliminate gossip or rumor mongering, but you can provide employees some response mechanisms to prepare them for when they are on the receiving end of gossip:

- "Why are you telling *me* this? Have you considered talking directly to the person with whom you have the problem?"

- "What you're telling me makes me very uncomfortable. Please don't say any more."

- "I wouldn't like being talked about this way. Would you?"

- "How do you know that the information you are repeating is even true? Did you see this yourself, or are you just spreading a rumor that could really hurt someone?"

- "I don't know if what you're saying is true or not, but it's certainly not very kind."

- "What you're saying about this person has nothing to do with work. It is really none of our business, and we shouldn't be talking about it."

- "Let's be loyal to those not present."

Gossip or rumor mongering can be mean-spirited, and it can destroy someone's reputation. As a manager, ensure you do not condone or participate in it. By actively listening to gossip, you are inadvertently enabling it. And under no circumstances should you ever bad-mouth one employee to another employee or violate personal confidences.

Packaging Your Ideas for Change

Whenever you introduce change, employees will naturally talk about it among themselves. Don't assume that your "great" idea for a change will go uncontested just because it's the right or the good thing to do. Anticipate and plan for resistance to your idea so that you can get employee ownership. Listed below are typical employee responses in defense of "keeping things the way they are." Before you present your change, make certain that you are prepared to address these concerns:

Concern About Having to Do Something New or Different:

- What's the need for change?
- We've always done it this way.
- What we're doing now is working, and we're satisfied.
- How do you know this will make things better?
- Have you assessed the possible side effects or the negative consequences of the change?

Fear of Change for the Sake of Change Itself:

- We have tried that before.
- Feels like "here we go again."
- By the time we change everything, there will be another change.

Fear of Failure:

- What new things will we have to learn, and will we get the resources to learn them?
- How much time will we have to learn this?
- I don't mind this change, but the others won't buy into it.

Concern About Practicality:

- This represents more work. Will it really help us?
- We are already overloaded. We don't have the time to do this.
- What can we give up?

Concern About Being Included:

- Will you listen to alternatives?
- Are we going to have input on this decision?

Direct, Overt Rejection:

- It won't work.
- We can't see the advantages.
- This will be a waste of time.

"Yes... But" Response:

- We're different/special; this should not apply to us.
- This will make everyone unhappy.
- It sounds good, but where is the evidence it's worked someplace else?

Concern About Control or Accountability:

- What if we refuse because we think this change is unwise/illegal/unsafe/unprofessional? What will be the consequences?
- Will we be responsible if it fails?

Employees will more readily accept change if they are:

- involved in the process
- asked to contribute their opinions and suggestions

- given reasons and advantages that will mitigate their uncertainty about the change

- provided honest communication, creating an atmosphere of trust

- respected for their feelings, even though they may oppose the change

- asked what assistance is necessary to facilitate their successful implementation of the change

- given appropriate recognition for their contribution in implementing the change

- given an explanation of the context and meaning for the change

Listed below is a checklist to determine if you have effectively addressed your employees' questions and concerns regarding any proposed change:

- Am I open to their opinions? Is there another way of doing this? If including employees in the decision-making process is not possible or appropriate, have I told them why the change is necessary?

- Am I being respectful and considerate? Is this how I would like to be treated?

- Have I given them adequate time to think about the implications of the change and how it will affect them?

- Is this change based on accurate information?

- Have I communicated my expectations regarding how employees should conduct themselves even if they may oppose the change?

- Have I demonstrated my belief in and commitment to the change?

- Am I flexible and adaptable? Do I admit mistakes and make corrections when appropriate?

- Do I understand the history of the group? How have they been treated before? Have they been deceived or hurt before?

- Are my deadlines realistic?

- Is this the best time?

- Have I provided them the necessary resources to succeed? Have I prepared them?

- Am I providing appreciation and recognition for those employees who are effectively implementing the change?

- Can I be counted on? Will I be there for them in the long run? Can they trust me?

- Am I modeling the attitude and conduct expected of employees, demonstrating effective listening, stress-reduction and conflict-management skills? Am I leading by example?

Many employees become paralyzed by the fear of change. They dwell on potential problems, and their constant worrying inhibits their job success and satisfaction. Following is a six-step coaching model to help employees manage their fear of the unknown (Chambers, 155):

Coaching Employees Through Change

1. **Identify the worst-case scenario.** Help employees articulate their specific concerns:

WHAT YOU ACCEPT IS WHAT YOU TEACH

- "What do you fear may happen?"

- "What is the worst possible thing that could happen?"

- "If this doesn't work well, what is the worst outcome you can imagine?"

2. **Summarize employees' articulated concerns back to them.** This helps them "hear" their fears void of emotion and judgment. This also demonstrates your interest and ensures the accuracy of your understanding:

- "I understand your concern is that...."

- "I'm hearing you say that you see the potential for...."

3. **Affirm the employee's thought process.** Acknowledge without necessarily agreeing. This aligns you with the employee's concerns:

- "I'm glad you shared this with me."

- "I would be concerned too if I thought that would happen."

- "I know this really worries you."

4. **Project the potential positive side of any change.** Help the employee consider a positive outcome:

- "Let's look at this another way. What is the best thing that could happen?"

- "Let's see if we can anticipate some positive outcomes."

- "If it goes as planned, what do you think some good results would be?"

5. **Help the employee gain some measure of control.** Develop an action plan for dealing with concerns:

   - "What can be done to minimize the chances that your worst fears will be realized?"

   - "How can we avoid allowing this negative outcome to occur?"

   - "What can we do now to plan for the worst-case scenario?"

6. **If the employee becomes convinced that he actually sees the bad starting to develop, make him part of the solution:**

   - "Interesting observation. What can we do to fix it?"

   - "What can we do to double-check or verify your suspicion?"

   - "If your observation is correct, what can we do to make sure we stop it now?"

It has been said that:

- 60 percent of our fears are totally unwarranted. They never come to pass.

- 20 percent of our fears are focused on our past, which is completely out of control. You can't change the past, so don't dwell on it.

- 10 percent of our fears are based on issues so petty that they make no lasting difference in our lives.

- Of the remaining 10 percent, only 4 to 5 percent could be considered justifiable.

This suggests that much of the time and energy we expend on fear-related thoughts are totally wasted. We allow ourselves to be held prisoner by our own unwarranted worries.

Ask employees to become aware of their own thoughts about change. Sometimes we don't have control of the change itself, but we do have control over our attitude about it. Consider these constructive thoughts about change:

- It is sometimes necessary to get out of our comfort zone, to learn a new skill, to try something different or look at things from a different perspective. As uncomfortable as it feels, changing is much better than getting stuck in behaviors or thoughts that no longer apply to the present situation.

- Sometimes not taking a risk, doing nothing, resisting or openly sabotaging a change becomes the far greater risk. After all, the change could lead to something better if we all do what is needed to make it work.

- Often, we can anticipate and plan for change. The handwriting is on the wall if only we stop to notice. Denying reality, even if we don't like the change, can be devastating to our job success, satisfaction and security.

- When we don't have control over what's happening, letting go and simply trusting what lies ahead can be very liberating. People are happiest when they are not dominated by fear or worry.

- When things get really crazy, it's helpful to maintain a benign amusement about what's happening. Perspective and a good sense of humor are vital for our mental health.

- When we change how we think, we change what we do. We can choose to believe that a particular change will harm us, and we will naturally resist it. Or we can choose to believe that the change has the potential to make things better and embrace the change by working for its success. Our positive or negative thoughts about change, therefore, can become self-fulfilling prophecies.

- If we spend less time complaining or worrying about a change and more time figuring out how we can make it work, we will have more positive outcomes. When we catch ourselves worrying, we need to replace the worry with a plan.

- Some fears about change should be respected as they keep us out of real danger. But many fears are irrational, and they paralyze us from responding in a constructive manner. Let's not complicate things. Let's keep life as simple as possible. If the change is outside our control, then we need to accept and adapt to it, be flexible and move on. But let's not play the role of victim as if we are captive and powerless in our present circumstances. We have choices to make, and not making a choice *is* a choice.

The only constant is change. This is the ultimate paradox. Life is like a roller coaster. It is full of unexpected turns, sudden drops, rises and breathtaking speed. Those who can enjoy the ride achieve the most satisfaction.

Notes:

ATTITUDE

The longer I live, the more I realize the impact of attitude on life. Attitude, to me, is more important than past, than education, than money, than circumstances, than failures, than success, than what other people think or say or do. It is more important than appearance, giftedness, or skill. It will make or break a company… a church… a home. The remarkable thing is we have a choice every day regarding the attitude we will embrace for that day. We cannot change our past… we cannot change the fact that people will act in a certain way. We cannot change the inevitable. The only thing we can do is play on the one string we have, and that is our attitude… I am convinced that life is 10 percent what happens to me and 90 percent how I react to it… We are in charge of our attitude.

Author Unknown

COACHING EMPLOYEES TO TAKE RESPONSIBILITY FOR THEIR ATTITUDE

We can't choose our parents, our genes or our upbringing. We have no control over our birth order or what sign we were born under. We all have limitations, whether lack of talent, financial resources or physical attributes. We are all on occasion thrust into challenging situations through no fault of our own. But we are always responsible for our *reaction* to what happens to us. In fact, we can never *not* be responsible for our reaction, regardless of circumstances.

Responsibility does not mean blame or guilt. It simply implies that even when provoked, we must ably respond to the situation and account for what we say or do. The freedom to choose without accepting personal responsibility for the consequences of our actions leads to a breakdown of civility and order.

Our attitude is a choice. The truth is that anyone, no matter how good the working conditions, can find a reason to have a negative attitude. And anyone, no matter how bad the circumstances, can find a way to maintain a positive attitude. Our attitude is of our own making and largely depends on these influences:

1. **What We Focus On:** Our attitude will likely suffer if we concentrate on everything that is frustrating or unfair and if we take for granted the positive aspects of the working condition. When we dwell on the negative, we feed it with energy. What we pay attention to only grows stronger.

2. **What We Think When Things Go Bad:** Many of the dissatisfiers at work are irritating, but they are not catastrophes. A catastrophe is the AIDS epidemic in Africa or a hurricane that wipes out a city. What most of us experience when things go wrong at work is frustrating, inconvenient and disappointing, but it is not disastrous. We must place things in proper perspective. Don't become a drama queen or king. Don't make mountains out of molehills or worry about things that have not yet happened (and may not ever happen). This only prevents us from living in the moment, recognizing and taking full advantage of what *is* positive in the work environment.

3. **Whom We Associate With:** If we spend all of our time with someone who is negative and angry, it is very possible that the person's unhappiness will begin to affect our own attitude. Misery likes company, and negativity is very contagious. The disgruntled co-worker *expects* that we join him in his griping and dumping. And if we are too satisfied with our job, there is something wrong with *us*: We are naive. We are in denial. We are apple polishers if we get along

too well with management. All of us are judged by the company we keep. Our associations are a reflection of our values. Choose wisely.

4. **Our Expectations:** One definition of conflict is "expectations not met." Therefore, when we are experiencing job-related frustrations, we must examine our expectations. Questions to ask include:

- What do we want, need or expect from this job/department/organization/co-worker?

- Are our expectations realistic given the inherent constraints and limitations (realities) of the workplace?

- If our expectations are reasonable, have we asked for what we want in a clear, concise and constructive manner? Are we packaging our ideas in a way that enables others to listen? Are we actively listening to others so that they are able to talk with us?

- Are we patient, or do we have a need for immediate gratification?

- Have we separated problems (obstacles to job satisfaction that can be resolved) from realities (obstacles that no one can do anything about)?

- If our expectations can't be met here, where can they be met? Are we willing to consider changing our shift, department, organization or career to meet our needs? If not, how can we best accept or adapt to these frustrations and focus on things that *are* within our control?

COACHING EMPLOYEES TO TAKE RESPONSIBILITY FOR THEIR ATTITUDE

- Are we willing to concentrate and take full advantage of what is working well within our department?

Happiness comes from taking pride in our work and seeing the positive results of our efforts. It comes from being a member of a dedicated, cohesive and successful work team. Regardless of work constraints or limitations, our primary focus should be on the contribution that we are making on behalf of the customers we serve.

If working full time, we spend one-half of our waking hours on the job. We probably spend more time with our co-workers than we do our immediate family. It should be a satisfying and fulfilling experience. But the secret to job happiness has less to do with the work environment than with making the right career choices.

The key is to first find a job that we are naturally good at. Work is so much easier when we are engaged in an activity that plays to our strengths. We are more likely to get the recognition we deserve, positive performance evaluations or merit increases when the job is a good match for our God-given talents.

The second key to job satisfaction is to find a job that we truly enjoy. It sometimes doesn't even feel like work when we love what we do. We don't resent the amount of time and effort we invest in the job when we truly care about the results of the activity.

It is difficult to determine which comes first: We generally like what we are good at, and we are good at what we like. It doesn't matter. The secret is to identify our strengths and desires, then find an organization that will pay us to do what comes naturally. The money will follow. And even if the job does not bring us great wealth, we will enjoy *inner affluence* because we are following our bliss.

There will always be aspects of the job that are frustrating and demanding. But we don't mind them so much when we love our work and care about the results of our efforts. To ensure that we have the right job, therefore, we must ask ourselves the following questions:

- What am I naturally good at? What aspects of my job are exceedingly difficult for me? Am I willing to do what it takes to improve?

- What do I enjoy most about my job? What aspects of the work do I enjoy least? Am I willing to perform these least desirable tasks in a pleasant and professional manner?

- What kind of job plays to my strengths?

- What kind of job would actually excite me?

- Where can I make the greatest contribution?

- What do I need to do to prepare for my ideal job? Am I prepared to make the sacrifices necessary to achieve my objective?

We should waste as little time as possible on improving our areas of low competence. Most of our energy should be devoted to cultivating and utilizing our strengths. And no matter how good we are as actors, if we really dislike our job, it shows. No matter how hard we try, people see through our disinterest, disdain or despair:

> A labor of love is the work we do not because we are paid but because of the satisfaction it provides. A labor of love cannot be indifferent work, for love cancels out indifference. It is done to the best of our ability because we want to give our best for its own sake. We care so much for what we do that we take the care to do it properly.

> When labor is *not* that of love, then how can
> we talk about it? Is it a labor of hate, is it work
> without care, is it something done without feel-
> ing? Is it utopian to think that we can love all
> our work? We cannot always find the perfect fit;
> sometimes the fit is fractured. But it is demeaning
> to think that we must separate labor and love. For
> work without love is servitude. (Zinni, 223)

Job success and satisfaction are fundamentally interconnected. The only truly effective employees are those working
at something they consider important. Ultimately, achievement is the essential precondition for both job satisfaction
and self-worth.

To maintain a positive attitude, we must also stop blam-
ing other people or circumstances. We should not wait for
positive change to occur. We should create it by acting in a
concrete manner that moves us closer to our objectives. We
should experiment with our behavior and examine the results. We must also do less of what doesn't work: If we keep
doing what we're doing with negative results, we will keep
getting more of the same results. So if we don't like what
we're getting, we must change what we're doing.

Finally, let's observe the actions of others we admire
most for their job confidence and interpersonal effectiveness, and model their behaviors. People who enjoy a positive attitude and who effectively manage change have these
qualities in common:

- They have a strong, healthy self-esteem.

- They take personal responsibility for themselves. They
  take control over what they think, do, say, and feel.

- They face obstacles and setbacks with courage. They accept changes that are outside their control, or they influence the outcome when possible. But they don't play the role of victim.

- They don't put things off. They don't wait around, wondering what to do. They find the answers they need and put themselves into motion. When they catch themselves obsessing over everything that can go wrong, they replace the worry with a plan.

- They get help when needed. They seek out others for support and advice on how to responsibly manage the situation.

- They see unwanted change and conflict as a natural and inherent part of life. They use them as potential catalysts for learning and growing.

- They make the choice to excel in times of difficulty. An accurate description of people who effectively respond to these challenges include such words as:

self-managed	confident
calm	levelheaded
optimistic	enthusiastic
determined	empathic
responsible	patient
open-minded	flexible
proactive	resilient
professional	passionate

Principles for People Development

Value people: This is an issue of my attitude

Commitment to people: This is an issue of my time

Integrity with people: This is an issue of my character

Standards for people: This is an issue of my vision

Influence over people: This is an issue of my leadership

John C. Maxwell

THE IMPORTANCE OF RECOGNITION

Some managers are quick to criticize yet reluctant to credit. They also embrace some dangerous misconceptions about employee recognition:

- I'm dealing with adults, not children. They should know when they are doing a good job. I shouldn't have to slobber all over them.

- Employees are getting paid to work. Why should I praise them for just doing their job?

- If I praise them too much, they will only want more money.

- Praise is overrated. You get more with the stick than you do with the carrot.

- An employee's performance should be perfect before he is recognized.

- There is *always* room for improvement. So I must
  continuously point out the performance deficiencies.
  Besides, I don't want employees to feel *too* good about
  their work. They may get complacent!

Some managers believe that there are a finite number
of compliments in the world. If they give a compliment to
one person, that's one fewer to give to someone else. These
managers believe that positive feedback must be provided
very cautiously and sparingly. Other managers are afraid
to recognize employees because they are embarrassed, or
they don't compliment because they never learned how to
do so. Still other managers don't receive much recognition
themselves. So they seem unwilling or unable to give it. As a
result, many employees are working in a state of psychological deprivation relative to positive feedback.

*Recognition, given the right way, for the right reasons, at the right
time, may be the most powerful tool available to a manager.* In fact,
you cannot give *too* much positive feedback to an employee
providing that you are sincere and the person deserves it.
Covey (1989) utilizes the Emotional Bank Account meta-
phor to impress the importance of recognition:

> In a financial bank account, we make deposits
> and build up a reserve from which we can make
> withdrawals whenever we need to. An emotional
> bank account is a metaphor that describes the
> amount of trust that is built up in a relationship.
> If I make deposits into this emotional bank with
> you through courtesy, kindness, honesty, and
> keeping my commitments to you, I build up a re-
> serve. Your trust towards me becomes higher, and
> then I can call upon that trust many times if I
> need to. I can make mistakes and that trust level,
> that emotional reserve, will compensate for it.

But, if I have a habit of showing discourtesy, disrespect, writing you off, overreacting or ignoring you, being arbitrary, or threatening you, eventually my emotional bank account is overdrawn. The trust level gets very low. I am walking on minefields with you. I have to be careful with everything I say. I have to measure every word. It's tension city. (p. 188)

In order to keep your emotional bank account solvent with employees, apply the following recognition principles:

1. **Learn to notice when the employee is doing something right.** It is a question of selective perception. If you look for the positive in people, the evidence is there to behold. Remember, that behavior which is reinforced usually is repeated. Equally important, you risk extinguishing the positive behavior by not recognizing it.

2. **Don't wait too long to compliment.** The best performance feedback is provided in a timely fashion, as soon as possible after the event occurs. If you wait too long to recognize someone, you might forget to compliment, or by the time you give it, the feedback will be too general and will have lost the desired effect.

3. **Be specific when you compliment someone.** Describe in concrete terms what you saw or heard and the positive impact the employee's behavior had on others. It's simply not enough to say, for example, "Good job." From the employee's point of view, it is certainly nice to hear that you are pleased with her work. But "Good job" is so general it doesn't tell the employee what she did to earn your praise. If she doesn't know what she did, how can she repeat it?

4. **Be pure in your reinforcement.** Stop after you give the compliment. Don't mix your messages by telling the employee what she could have done better:

"You did well. But next time I want you to...."

"That was great. But if you only would have...."

If you mix your messages, the employee may only remember the "but" of the statement and forget the compliment. And, if you engage in this practice too often, the employee will suspect that the only reason you gave the compliment was to give the criticism.

5. **Don't wait for performance perfection before you compliment.** There is always *something* an employee can do better. You can positively shape and influence an employee's progress by recognizing his success in incremental terms. When you recognize the small steps of improvement, you are building confidence and encouraging the employee to continue in a positive direction.

6. **Compliment in front of others.** This practice has the potential of magnifying the positive impact, and the employee's actions can serve as a positive example for co-workers to emulate. But use caution: some employees are embarrassed by receiving public praise, or they may be resented by other members of the department. Know your team culture and utilize discretion.

7. **Encourage others to compliment.** You should not be the only person responsible for recognizing positive behaviors within the work team. Communicate your expectation that it is everyone's job to

create a positive work environment. When a co-worker or customer praises an employee to you, ask if he or she would like to personally thank the employee or write a note recognizing the employee's outstanding service.

8. **Celebrate group successes.** Be sure to recognize team effort whenever employees go above and beyond to meet or exceed customer expectations. Thank the group as a whole, for example, by purchasing pizza or donuts or by sending personalized thank-you notes to all employees involved in the collaborative effort. By recognizing group effort, you are reinforcing the values of effective teamwork and enhancing team morale in the process.

The Power of Thank-You Notes

Sending personalized thank-you notes is one of the most powerful strategies to recognize exemplary employee performance. You should consider sending a note of thanks to an employee whenever:

- *You directly observe* the person going above and beyond to exceed a customer's or co-worker's needs.

- A *co-worker tells you* about a person who went above and beyond to exceed customer or peer expectations.

- A *customer tells you* about a person who went above and beyond to exceed expectations.

- A *customer satisfaction survey specifically names a person* who wowed a customer with high quality service.

- *Two or more employees cooperate with one another* to exceed a customer's expectations, or they demonstrate outstanding teamwork within or between departments.

- *A person advances an excellent idea* to improve the quality of customer service or employee relations, enhances the level of technical competence or advances a way to make or save money for the organization.

Whenever you send a thank-you note to an employee, you should also send copies to your own manager and a human resource representative, requesting that it be placed in the employee's personnel file. You can also ask your manager to write the employee a letter, thanking the person on behalf of the organization for conduct consistent with the organization's mission, vision and values. And remember to be as specific in your thank-you notes as you would be with verbal recognition.

Regardless of what form your recognition takes, be certain to individualize your compliments. What is reinforcing to one person may be aversive to someone else. For example, giving one employee more responsibility as a reward for outstanding performance may be truly appreciated. It shows that you trust the person and value his quality of work. Giving another employee additional responsibility as a reward for good performance may be viewed as a punishment. The employee might think, "Is this the reward I get for doing good work... *more* work? Thanks, but no thanks. I'm perfectly happy with what I'm doing now." Therefore, try to tailor your recognition to meet the specific needs and desires of your employees.

The form on page 150 lists what employees say they want from their job. Ask your employees to complete this form; then interview them to determine their specific expectations of you and of the organization.

For example, the first item on the list is "Accurate and Timely Feedback." If an employee rates this category as Very Important, ask how often he would like to receive performance feedback so that there are no surprises on the year-end performance appraisal. If an employee rates "Support" as Very Important, request that he provide you examples of what he means by support. Does it mean investigating and backing him up when criticized by a customer? Does it mean providing the necessary materials and supplies to perform his job?

This form also gives you the opportunity to informally negotiate with employees which of their needs are within or outside your control to meet. For example, an employee may say that her definition of "Support" is that you personally roll up your sleeves and get your hands dirty whenever the need exists. Your response might be, "I am always willing to help out when I can, and when I'm aware of the need. But I can't become part of the staffing pattern, because I also have many administrative tasks to complete and meetings to attend."

Or the employee may indicate that she wants more "Autonomy and Control" in her job. But she may not be ready to assume more independence of action due to specific skill deficits or her lack of follow-through on assigned tasks. This form provides you the opportunity to communicate to the employee what she must demonstrate before you can give her more autonomy and control over her job.

WHAT DO YOU WANT FROM YOUR JOB?

Please rate the job-related items listed below according to their importance to you.

Job-Related Item	Very Important	Somewhat Important	Unimportant
Accurate and timely feedback	☐	☐	☐
Appreciation for work well done	☐	☐	☐
Attention	☐	☐	☐
Autonomy/control over one's job	☐	☐	☐
Being treated fairly	☐	☐	☐
Challenging work	☐	☐	☐
Clear policies and procedures	☐	☐	☐
Clear goals	☐	☐	☐
Flexible job duties	☐	☐	☐
Flexible schedule	☐	☐	☐
Good interpersonal relationships	☐	☐	☐
Good supervision	☐	☐	☐
Good working conditions	☐	☐	☐
Interesting work	☐	☐	☐
Job security	☐	☐	☐
Leisure time/work/life balance	☐	☐	☐
More responsibility	☐	☐	☐
Opportunity for advancement	☐	☐	☐
Opportunity to learn and grow	☐	☐	☐
Opportunity to make a difference	☐	☐	☐
Participation in decisions	☐	☐	☐
Pay	☐	☐	☐
Praise/recognition	☐	☐	☐
Respect	☐	☐	☐
Support	☐	☐	☐
Sharing information	☐	☐	☐
Teamwork/cooperation within and between departments	☐	☐	☐
Others:	☐	☐	☐

Note: A variation might be to ask employees how much of each item they are currently receiving versus the amount they would like to receive (i.e., My manager: (a) could provide much more, (b) could provide a little more, (c) is providing all that is needed). Or you may want to have employees rank the items they checked as Very Important from most to least important.

Regarding pay as a motivator, employees judge the amount of their income against three barometers:

- Is it fair considering the amount of effort required to do the job?

- How does my pay compare with that of my co-workers considering the amount of work they have or how well they are executing their jobs?

- How does my pay compare with that of employees in other organizations engaged in similar jobs?

If these three factors are generally acceptable to employees, then pay does not become the primary motivator for doing outstanding work. The psychosocial factors become more important. Money is critical and necessary, but it consistently rates well down the list of what matters most to employees. Overwhelmingly, the important motivators are intrinsic to the work itself and the quality of the manager-employee relationship.

Therefore, don't use pay as the primary lever to get better performance. It takes no time, talent or courage to say to an employee, "If you improve the quality of your work, I'll give you more money." Money will focus the employee on the extrinsic reward instead of the intrinsic motivation of taking pride in one's work. As a manager, you probably have limited control over how much you can pay someone based upon merit. Therefore, you might as well concentrate on those motivating factors over which you do have direct influence:

- creating a relationship based upon honesty, trust and goodwill

- providing challenging, yet achievable performance goals

- ensuring that employees know where they stand with you through ongoing performance feedback

- providing sincere and appropriate recognition

So much money is thrown at the challenge of holding on to good employees in the form of better pay and perks when in the end, turnover is primarily a managerial issue. Buckingham and Coffman (1999, 33), in their research on employee morale, suggest that if you set clear expectations and know, respect and invest in people, then an employee will probably forgive the organization for its lack of a profit sharing program. But if the manager-employee relationship is fractured, there is no amount of money that will persuade someone to stay. From an employee's perspective, it is better to work for an effective manager in an old-fashioned organization than for a terrible manager in an organization that pays well. Therefore, pay employees commensurate with their value in the marketplace, keep the lines of communication open at all times and then do whatever you can to keep their minds off the money!

An Exercise to Strengthen Employee Relationships

1. Using the form on page 155, identify those employees who wield the most informal influence on your team. Although these employees don't hold official position power, others turn to them to help shape attitudes and opinions, positive or negative.

2. Identify the sources of influence for these employees. Why is it that they enjoy so much credibility with other members on your team? What personal attributes make others gravitate toward them?

3. Develop a management strategy to establish a better working relationship with each of these employees because these are the team members who can most help or hurt the accomplishment of your goals.

For the negative opinion leaders, develop a strategy to:

- co-opt them or neutralize their negative energy

- turn their cynicism into healthy skepticism

- include them in decision-making processes so that they feel a part of the solutions to problems they identify

- demonstrate that you are not working at counter-purposes with them, that you are aligned with their self-interest

- recognize and build on their strengths instead of exclusively focusing on their shortcomings

- let them know that you care

For those positive opinion leaders, develop a strategy to:

- place them in a more pivotal position to make a difference

- better utilize their particular strengths and interests for the benefit of the work team

- provide them with a means to be more proactive in exercising their positive influence

Make an effort to spend one-on-one quality time with all employees to get to know them better and to develop a relationship of trust and openness. Get past any feelings of frustration and bitterness toward them. Try to start a new day.

Use these meetings to communicate your empathy with their concerns. Demonstrate that you understand why they might be ambivalent or resistant to your goals. Their perceptions, right or wrong, are real. You can't simply dismiss them. Be prepared to informally negotiate with them what you can do to make their jobs easier, more satisfying and effective.

Make a commitment to keep open the lines of communication. Request that they do not assume malicious intent if you inadvertently do something that upsets them. Instead, request that they provide you feedback at the earliest opportunity in a direct, honest and respectful manner.

You improve team morale by "working" your department one employee at a time. The objective here is not to become more popular or liked. You are engaged in these activities because good relationships grease the results channels. Good relationships facilitate individual job success and satisfaction. Good relationships make it easier to resolve conflicts that will inevitably occur within your department.

Strengthening Employee Relationships

List Your Employee Opinion Leaders	Identify Whether the Employee Is a Positive Opinion Leader or Negative Opinion Leader	Identify Source of Employee's Influence/Personal Attributes Leading to Credibility Within Team	Develop Your Management Strategy for Strengthening the Employee Relationship

There is no more noble occupation in this world than
to assist another human being to succeed.

_____

Alan Loy McGinnis

13

ACCOUNTABILITY STARTS AT NEW EMPLOYEE ORIENTATION

In the dictionary, *orientation* means to effectively adapt to one's new surroundings, to become secure in one's bearings, grounded in a new reality. Unfortunately, because their departmental orientation was not well planned or executed, many new employees feel just the opposite: confused, unfocused, bewildered and overwhelmed.

Orienting new employees to their department and jobs may be one of the most neglected managerial functions within organizations. Do you set up new employees for frustrations or failure?

- Does your department orientation process indicate to the new employee that she is not valued as a person and as a valuable resource?

- How many times when your new employees arrived in your department has everyone been too busy to greet them, help integrate them into the psychosocial milieu, direct their activities or teach them their new job?

- Does your orientation process add up to information overload, making the new employee feel like he has to know and do everything immediately in order to be accepted or approved of by others?

- Do your long-term employees eat their young by refusing to answer the new employee's questions or ignoring his requests for help?

To empathize with new employees, try to remember *your* first day on the job:

- Were you confident or anxious?

- Were you made to feel welcome? Was someone waiting for you when you arrived on the work unit the first day?

- Were people aware of you coming in as a new hire? Were you introduced around?

- Did you get the information you needed to effectively perform the job? Did you understand what was expected of you?

- Did you have the opportunity to ask questions about the work environment, policies, procedures and department protocols, or did you have to learn them on your own?

- What resources were made available to you?

In summary, was your new employee orientation process well orchestrated to facilitate your success and to confirm that you made the right decision to accept the job? Critical to a new employee's job success and satisfaction is the amount of time and effort that you personally put into the orientation process. You want to help the new employee get up to speed quickly and thoroughly. You want to make her feel welcome and accepted as a vital member of the work team. You want to reduce the anxiety that results from entering into an unfamiliar situation. You want to offer a learning environment where the new employee can build on her strengths and shore up her weaknesses. Above all, you want to confirm for the new employee that she made the right decision to work in your department. You want the employee to come away with these perceptions:

- The department has a friendly and supportive work environment.

- Positive things are said about the work and the department. People actually like what they are doing.

- Employees appear to have a good work and service ethic. They are focused on the right things.

- People understand the nature of their interdependency. There is a constructive relationship between the manager and staff, between shifts and work units. People are facilitating each other's success and satisfaction.

To achieve these positive outcomes, you must effectively manage the following critical steps in the new employee orientation process:

1. Pre-Arrival Activities:

- Contact the new hire with employment and arrival information. E-mail, telephone or send a welcome letter to the new employee, confirming when and where to report.

- Send a notice to all current staff announcing the new employee's arrival with an orientation schedule that has his specific roles and responsibilities. State your firm expectation that it is every employee's responsibility to create a positive first impression and to set up the person for success. The pre-arrival memo should include:
  - the employee's name (with nickname preference if indicated)
  - the starting date
  - the office telephone number (if applicable)
  - a brief description of the new employee's education, experience, background and other information that the person would like to share
  - a request for staff to introduce themselves and to mention how they will be working with the new employee

Convey a level of excitement and enthusiasm about the new working relationship and the confidence that the new employee will be a welcome addition to the department.

Before the employee arrives on the first day, you should also develop an orientation plan, with a schedule of activities that includes:

- *who* specifically will be involved in the orientation process

- *what* each person's responsibilities will be

- *when* each step in the orientation process will begin

- *where* the orientation will be held

If appropriate, assign a mentor whose responsibilities will be to facilitate the new employee's comfort, answer questions and become a sounding board, advisor and advocate. But don't choose just anyone to serve as a mentor. Make certain that this person:

- has a positive attitude and is a good role model

- is proud of the department and has good things to say abut the organization

- is someone not caught up in departmental politics, turf battles and personality conflicts

- is a competent performer

- has patience and is nonjudgmental with a new department member

- is someone who will listen objectively, evaluate and provide encouragement

- has the time and flexibility to train and develop the new employee

- is someone who is trained in the skills of mentorship

If there is no one within your department who meets the above criteria, then you might need to take on some of these responsibilities yourself. Whatever it takes, don't let the new employee wallow in ambiguity, isolation or paranoia. It is unethical and costly.

2. First-Day Activities:

Your role during the orientation process must be an active one. Your calendar should be open to devote as much time as possible to the new employee:

- Be there to greet the employee.

- Give the employee his orientation schedule with a folder in which to place additional material.

- Make critical introductions by walking the new employee around or having staff meet in a group at a specific time and place.

- Offer refreshments. *Celebrate his arrival.*

- Take the new employee to lunch or arrange for someone else to do so.

- Assign a meaningful work assignment for the first few days, one in which the person can succeed.

It's all right if you're going to delegate some of these responsibilities, but do not assign anyone to orient the new employee until you have made the initial contact and have established a plan for the days ahead.

Utilize a new employee orientation checklist to document the presentation of department policies and procedures, specific job responsibilities and expected behaviors, including standards of conduct to support customer service and teamwork. Review the job description and performance appraisal form(s) so that the employee understands the criteria by which she will be judged. Discuss anything else that helps explain, "Here's how we do things around here:"

- hours and days the employee will work
- shift schedules, posting of schedules and shift change requests, if applicable
- coffee breaks and meal periods (length and times)
- holidays (scheduling and eligibility)
- vacations and personal days
- importance of attendance, how and when to report absences
- completion of time cards and clocking in (how and when)
- distribution of paychecks
- amount and types of premiums and bonuses available, if applicable
- safety requirements, including department fire procedures, disaster plans, incident reporting, illness and injury report forms (when and how to complete them)
- tour of offices and the facility

Of course, no orientation process would be complete without an individual needs assessment and performance development plan tailored to the exact specifications of the new employee. This plan should build on the new employee's identified strengths and should address any skill set deficiencies. The new employee should be made aware of department in-service education programs, the organization's continuing education offerings and certification, registration and licensure requirements, if applicable.

3. First Two Weeks:

A performance agreement with the new hire should be established that includes:

- key results areas to be achieved (conditions of employment), such as outstanding customer service, effective teamwork, continuous quality improvement and fiscal responsibility

- standards of performance: the indicators of success (evaluation criteria) to evaluate quality of work, including monitoring and evaluation methods to be utilized

- how often you and the employee will meet to assess progress and to maintain a healthy ongoing dialogue

- available resources to facilitate the employee's success and inherent limitations that may serve as obstacles to quality performance

- the amount of autonomy and authority to perform tasks

- recognition for achieving results and consequences for failure to meet expectations

- formal performance review dates

During the new employee orientation process, regularly assess the person's degree of satisfaction and ask for input on how the department can be improved. Utilize the new employee as an internal consultant by asking some of the following questions:

- How do we compare to what we said when we hired you?

- What do we do well?

- Who are some people who have been especially helpful to you during this time?

- What are some ways we can improve on customer service, teamwork or technical competence? How can we make or save money or utilize our resources more effectively?

- If you were in a position to change anything, what would it be?

- At your previous place of employment, what are some of the things that they did that we could implement here?

- Is anything here aversive to you that, if not corrected, might cause you to leave?

- Would you make the same decision to accept this job if you knew then what you know now?

- As your manager, is there anything you would like me to do differently that would make your job easier, more satisfying or effective?

- Are there any questions that I can answer for you now?

Throughout the new employee's first 90 days and beyond, stay focused on what the employee wants most from you: a good relationship, your accessibility and approachability, your support and advocacy, your appreciation and recognition for the contribution that she is making. Above all, the new employee needs to see you as someone who is vested in her success and looking out for her best interests. A well-structured, thorough new employee orientation process will go a long way to meeting these expectations.

Delegating Assignments to New Employees

1. Assessment:

- Identify what needs to be accomplished.

- Decide which of your responsibilities can't be delegated and what tasks can/should be delegated.

- Assess the new employee's workload, availability and confidence to accept the responsibility.

- Determine if the assignment is a good match for the employee's knowledge, skills, attitude and interests.

2. Planning:

- Schedule the assignment, making certain that the employee understands the importance of the task, the indicators of success (what the results will look like if the assignment is successfully completed), time frames, monitoring and evaluation methods to be used, recognition and consequences for meeting objectives.

- Discuss strategies for accomplishing the task. Whenever possible, allow the employee the opportunity to identify the methods by which the assignment will be completed. Unless there is only one way to proceed, provide for diversity of style and approach within the context of safety and professional standards and ethical and legal considerations.

- When appropriate, ask the employee to develop a method and timetable for you to review or negotiate before work begins.

- Ensure that the employee understands his level of authority to act or make decisions.

- If applicable, establish formats for training and ongoing coaching to facilitate employee success.

- Discuss the amount and frequency of performance feedback so that the employee is kept on track.

- Ensure that the employee understands the resources available to accomplish the task.

- Allow the employee to ask questions, clarify role and responsibilities, and share concerns. Take the necessary time up front. The investment will pay dividends in the long term.

- Assess the employee's understanding and ownership of the assignment. Observe his nonverbal behaviors (such as eye contact and facial expression), level of enthusiasm and confidence.

- Secure the employee's commitment to complete the task in accordance with established standards.

- Ensure that all relevant co-workers become aware of the delegation and provide their complete cooperation.

3. Evaluating Outcomes:

- Your amount of inspection largely depends on the level of trust you have in the employee and her own self-confidence to complete the task. Create tighter controls for less experienced, mature employees. Allow greater freedom for more experienced, skilled and self-managed employees.

- Provide ongoing evaluative feedback. Discuss progress and outcomes. When the task is completed, allow the employee to critique her own performance, including what she did well and what she would do differently next time.

- Recognize achievement. Be timely and specific in your praise.

- Level with the employee if positive outcomes are not achieved. Allow the employee to learn and develop through the experience. Mete out appropriate consequences if the failure was primarily caused by a poor attitude or lack of trying.

- Always hold employees accountable for honoring their commitments and following through on agreements.

Access to power must be confined to those
who are not in love with it.

_____

Plato

EXAMINING YOUR LEADERSHIP STYLE: AN AUDIT OF BEST PRACTICES

The following pages contain a summary of ten managerial activities that are essential for effectively managing performance and holding people accountable for results. Evaluate yourself relative to how well you perform each function and, as appropriate, make a commitment for positive change.

Leadership Responsibility #1:

Communicate a vision and set of values for my department and hold myself accountable through "leadership by example."

Indicators of Successful Performance:	How well do I perform in this leadership function?	What do I need to start doing (do more of) or stop doing (do less of)?
I have identified and communicated to employees what I "stand for" and will never compromise regardless of circumstance.	☐ Quite well ☐ OK ☐ Need to work on this	
I have aligned my time and activities with what I value. My values are reflected in my calendar book and what I talk about with employees. I attend to what is most important to move the department closer to my vision. I am focused on what is really important.	☐ Quite well ☐ OK ☐ Need to work on this	
I consistently demonstrate courtesy, respect and concern toward employees. I model the attitudes and behavior expected in others. I lead by example.	☐ Quite well ☐ OK ☐ Need to work on this	

Leadership Responsibility #2:

Translate my vision and values into specific, behaviorally concise expectations and monitor/evaluate outcomes.

Indicators of Successful Performance:	How well do I perform in this leadership function?	What do I need to start doing (more of) or stop doing (less of)?
I have developed and communicated performance expectations (with employee input) that are specific and concise. Standards of performance for customer service, teamwork, competency and fiscal responsibility are observable, quantifiable or verifiable so that they can be monitored and evaluated.	☐ Quite well ☐ OK ☐ Need to work on this	
I consistently inspect whether employees are meeting my expectations for customer service, teamwork, competency and fiscal responsibility.	☐ Quite well ☐ OK ☐ Need to work on this	
My monitoring and evaluation strategies provide me timely and specific data enabling me to identify those employees who are meeting/not meeting performance expectations.	☐ Quite well ☐ OK ☐ Need to work on this	
I share results with employees and have an action plan for continuous quality improvement.	☐ Quite well ☐ OK ☐ Need to work on this	

Leadership Responsibility #3:

Provide positive feedback, recognition and rewards on both an individual and a team basis to reinforce commendable actions.

Indicators of Successful Performance:	How well do I perform in this leadership function?	What do I need to start doing (more of) or stop doing (less of)?
I acknowledge the good performance of all individuals within my department by providing direct/timely positive feedback whenever warranted.	☐ Quite well ☐ OK ☐ Need to work on this	
I write formal commendations (with copy to employee file) whenever a person demonstrates outstanding performance.	☐ Quite well ☐ OK ☐ Need to work on this	
I regularly organize group celebrations when the team goes above and beyond the call of duty, solves a challenging problem, effectively manages a difficult conflict, etc.	☐ Quite well ☐ OK ☐ Need to work on this	
I take advantage of holidays, birthdays, employee events and professional association weeks to celebrate/socialize.	☐ Quite well ☐ OK ☐ Need to work on this	
I regularly use the organization's formal reward system, including: _____ _____ _____	☐ Quite well ☐ OK ☐ Need to work on this	

Leadership Responsibility #4:

Coaching, counseling and disciplining employees when performance expectations are not met, up to and including discharge.

Indicators of Successful Performance:	How well do I perform in this leadership function?	What do I need to start doing (more of) or stop doing (less of)?
I level with (confront) employees in a direct, honest, respectful and timely basis when expectations are not met. I am specific and behaviorally concise when giving performance feedback.	☐ Quite well ☐ OK ☐ Need to work on this	
I make the time to meet with employees in need of coaching to improve their quality of performance. When appropriate, I develop formal performance improvement action plans that document specific expectations, needs for improvement, potential consequences and resources to facilitate employee success.	☐ Quite well ☐ OK ☐ Need to work on this	
I am honest with employees on their performance reviews. My assessment is an accurate reflection of their performance quality.	☐ Quite well ☐ OK ☐ Need to work on this	

(Continued on next page)

(Continued from previous page)

Indicators of Successful Performance:	How well do I perform in this leadership function?	What do I need to start doing (more of) or stop doing (less of)?
After providing performance feedback, I follow through by inspecting whether positive change has occurred. I provide recognition for improvement or mete out consequences for continued failure to meet expectations.	☐ Quite well ☐ OK ☐ Need to work on this	
I ultimately discharge employees who lack the skill or will to meet key performance expectations following ethical/legal guidelines and personnel policies within my organization.	☐ Quite well ☐ OK ☐ Need to work on this	

Leadership Responsibility #5:

Regularly listen to employees, viewing them as internal customers, securing their input when decisions or changes are made.

Indicators of Successful Performance:	How well do I perform in this leadership function?	What do I need to start doing (more of) or stop doing (less of)?
I make the time to listen to the views of my employees on an individual or collective basis on how the quality of work (or work life) can be improved.	☐ Quite well ☐ OK ☐ Need to work on this	
I regularly ask employees for their input into my decision making process on changes that directly impact their work. I test out ideas with them and incorporate their thoughts into my final decision whenever possible.	☐ Quite well ☐ OK ☐ Need to work on this	
I have created a communication environment free of retribution so that employees can play the role of loyal devil's advocate without fear of retaliation.	☐ Quite well ☐ OK ☐ Need to work on this	
I help employees separate problems (that can be solved) from realities (obstacles to success that can't be overcome because they are outside my direct control to impact). I develop action plans to solve the problems, follow through, give status reports and get closure on issues.	☐ Quite well ☐ OK ☐ Need to work on this	

Leadership Responsibility #6:

Share information with employees, recognizing their "need to know" and be a part of the big picture.

Indicators of Successful Performance:	How well do I perform in this leadership function?	What do I need to start doing (more of) or stop doing (less of)?
I take the time at staff meetings or use other forms of communication to share with employees the following: • organizational goals/priorities with progress reports • budgetary issues • industry trends • what can be shared from management meetings • activities in which I am engaged when not present in department • what I learn from workshops/retreats/books • what is happening outside my work unit, department and other parts of the organization • _____	☐ Quite well ☐ OK ☐ Need to work on this	
I regularly ask my employees what they would like to know or have clarified in order to curb rumors and allow people to check out assumptions. My employees see the "big picture" and are not operating in a vacuum.	☐ Quite well ☐ OK ☐ Need to work on this	

Leadership Responsibility #7:

Train and develop employees to "set them up" for success.

Indicators of Successful Performance:	How well do I perform in this leadership function?	What do I need to start doing (more of) or stop doing (less of)?
I regularly help my employees assess their own competencies and provide learning opportunities to improve their performance.	☐ Quite well ☐ OK ☐ Need to work on this	
Employees are held accountable for attending programs and for applying what they have learned.	☐ Quite well ☐ OK ☐ Need to work on this	
I take interest in and facilitate my employees' career development/personal growth.	☐ Quite well ☐ OK ☐ Need to work on this	

Leadership Responsibility #8:

Ensure seamless service by promoting team building within and between departments.

Indicators of Successful Performance:	How well do I perform in this leadership function?	What do I need to start doing (more of) or stop doing (less of)?
I have developed protocols for problem solving and conflict management so that issues are addressed at the earliest and most appropriate levels. I facilitate direct and respectful communication among employees, and discourage aggressive or passive-aggressive behaviors.	☐ Quite well ☐ OK ☐ Need to work on this	
I am seen as manager of *all* my employees, representing equally each job category, shift and work unit within my department. I am not perceived as identifying or playing favorites with one person or group over another. I bring people together to discuss how they can facilitate each other's job success and satisfaction.	☐ Quite well ☐ OK ☐ Need to work on this	
I do whatever is possible to ensure that my department is working collaboratively with other work units. I don't hesitate to cross department lines to solve problems. I cast a positive spin when my employees question/criticize another area. I don't join in on the griping.	☐ Quite well ☐ OK ☐ Need to work on this	

Leadership Responsibility #9:

Serve as an ally and politician for employees.

Indicators of Successful Performance:	How well do I perform in this leadership function?	What do I need to start doing (more of) or stop doing (less of)?
I stand up for my employees when they are wrongfully or inappropriately criticized by others. I encourage my employees to support themselves if verbally abused, providing they respond in a constructive, assertive manner.	☐ Quite well ☐ OK ☐ Need to work on this	
I stand by my manager and support organizational decisions. I help employees gain an understanding and commitment to some of the difficult/unpopular decisions made by upper level management.	☐ Quite well ☐ OK ☐ Need to work on this	
I do everything in my power to access resources from the organization to facilitate my employees' success, i.e. materials and supplies, equipment, appropriate staffing to match the workload, compensation, etc. I am an advocate for my employees' concerns. I watch their backs.	☐ Quite well ☐ OK ☐ Need to work on this	

Leadership Responsibility #10:

Make effective hiring and promotion decisions and conduct a thorough department orientation for new employees.

Indicators of Successful Performance:	How well do I perform in this leadership function?	What do I need to start doing (more of) or stop doing (less of)?
When position openings exist, I don't panic, rush to judgment and hire quickly to secure a warm body.	☐ Quite well ☐ OK ☐ Need to work on this	
When interviewing candidates for employment or promotion, in addition to assessing their technical competence, I ask questions to evaluate their work and service ethic, intrinsic motivation, teamwork, conflict and change management skills.	☐ Quite well ☐ OK ☐ Need to work on this	
When a person is hired, I conduct a comprehensive orientation which addresses not only the technical skills/knowledge required to perform the job, but also the psychosocial needs of the new employee. I provide: • my time, attention and feedback • an appropriate welcome on first day • introductions to staff members and others • tour of unit/department • assignment of a mentor/ preceptor with a positive attitude • orientation to customer service and teamwork standards • _____	☐ Quite well ☐ OK ☐ Need to work on this	

First Do No Harm

Employees will follow your lead by the example you set:

- If you utilize your employees as a sounding board to criticize another manager or department, employees will be less willing to fully cooperate with those individuals.

- If you frequently lose your temper when under stress, employees will more likely violate rules of civility during difficult situations.

- If you fail to execute your own management responsibilities such as conducting timely and thoughtful performance evaluations, employees will be less committed to achieving outstanding results.

Listed below are ten management behaviors most troubling to employees. Use this as a checklist. If asked, would your employees mark Yes or No to the following statements?

My Manager:

Yes No

1. Does not provide timely and appropriate ☐ ☐ employee recognition; fails to encourage and hold everyone accountable to high performance standards.

2. Is not visible or accessible to employees; ☐ ☐ is too engaged in work that requires being away from the day-to-day activities of the department; doesn't really understand our problems.

Yes No

3. Is not supportive. Doesn't stand up for em- ☐ ☐
   ployees when criticized by others even when
   our actions are justifiable; doesn't "watch
   our back;" takes credit when things are going well, blames us when things go bad.

4. Is verbally abusive: yells, swears, calls us ☐ ☐
   names, interrupts; criticizes us in eyesight
   or earshot of customers and co-workers; is
   not composed in stressful situations.

5. Rarely asks us for our ideas before a change ☐ ☐
   is made that directly impacts our work;
   keeps us in the dark regarding what's going
   on outside our department.

6. Blames/discredits us without first listening to ☐ ☐
   our side when administering corrective action (accuses first and asks questions later).

7. Violates confidences; bad-mouths one em- ☐ ☐
   ployee to another; shares content of private meetings such as counseling sessions,
   appraisals or disciplinary actions; uses us
   as a sounding board to criticize upper level
   management decisions.

8. Accords certain employees preferential ☐ ☐
   treatment; favors one person or group over
   another; maintains close personal friendship
   to the exclusion of other team members.

Yes No

9. Is subject to mood swings, unpredictable ☐ ☐
from day to day, hour to hour; is warm,
considerate, and engaging one minute,
bites your head off the next; displaces frustrations onto employees when problems
occur in his personal or professional life.

10. Does not model the positive attitude or be- ☐ ☐
havior expected of us; doesn't keep promises or honor commitments; doesn't follow
through or achieve closure on issues; his
word is not his bond; we can't trust what
our manager says.

Based upon this assessment of what employees perceive,
what are you going to start (do more of) or stop (do less of) to
better meet employees' perceived needs and expectations?

Questions for Establishing an Effective Leadership Style

1. Why is role modeling the attitudes and behaviors expected in others the highest form of leadership?

2. People don't care how much you know until they
know how much you care. What are some ways that
you can show people you care about them?

3. If you have an employee who is a negative opinion
maker, how do you deal with the situation without
making the employee a victim?

4. All great leaders possess two things: They know where they are going, and they are able to persuade people to follow. What are ways a leader can communicate a vision for the work unit and secure employee buy-in?

5. Employees need to know what is expected of them in specific and behaviorally concise ways. They need to know the criteria by which they will be evaluated. How does a leader develop and articulate these standards in a way that employees understand and take ownership?

6. How can you involve others in your decision-making processes so that they feel more responsible for positive outcomes?

7. Everybody needs information to do their work. We are so in need of this resource that if we can't get the facts, we make them up. When rumors or gossip get out of hand, it's always a sign that people lack honest, meaningful information. How does a leader keep employees informed with timely, accurate and relevant information? What do you inform your employees about?

8. What does it mean to "set someone up for success?" What are some ways you could do that as a leader?

9. How does a leader create communication formats with employees to ensure that there is effective cooperation and coordination between shifts, job classifications and work units?

10. How does a leader communicate to employees difficult and unpopular decisions made from above with which the leader does not even agree? How

does a leader demonstrate support, serve as an ally and politician for employees yet identify with and remain loyal to upper level management?

11. Think about the different bosses (or coaches, teachers, ministry leaders, etc.) that you've had in the past. How would you describe the worst one? How about the best one?

Examining Your Leadership Vision and Values

1. What do you want to have accomplished when you step away from this position? What do you want people to say about you? What will be your legacy? Focus on employee and customer perceptions, results accomplished, values demonstrated.

2. What is the most important role you can play within this work unit/department to create a positive work environment that facilitates people's job success and satisfaction?

3. How specifically would you have to think, speak and act in order to bring this vision into being? What habits would you need to cultivate, and what habits would you have to delete from your present work style to live out this vision? What activities (actual daily choices), attitudes and concrete accomplishments would you achieve if you worked as if this vision was of utmost importance to you? How can you best use your time?

4. What obstacles (internal resistances or external constraints) stand in the way of your making these

changes? What action steps will you take to over-come or at least minimize these obstacles?

5. Have you identified an internal coach or other re-source whom you can use as a sounding board to guide you through the challenges ahead?

A Summary of Accountability Strategies

- Don't wait too long to address dysfunctional behaviors. Negativity is very contagious.

- Focus on specific behaviors (not personality, attitudes or beliefs) and the negative impact of an employee's actions on others.

- Describe specifically what the employee needs to start doing (do more of) or stop doing (do less of) to meet your expectations.

- Immediately address the employee's defensiveness about your performance feedback, particularly if he displays aggressive or passive-aggressive words or behavior.

- Articulate consequences for the employee if expectations are not met.

- Offer employees resources that will help them succeed.

- Monitor and evaluate progress. If behavior improves, recognize it. If it doesn't, follow your organizational corrective action process.

- Document all relevant conversations.

- Allow employees to play the role of loyal devil's advocate by creating a communication environment free of retribution, but insist that employees are constructive and collaborative in the process. Address system barriers that serve as an impediment to employee success and satisfaction to eliminate legitimate causes of employee negativity.

- Don't blame or punish the entire department for the negative behaviors of one or some of its members. Hold individuals accountable.

- Establish rules of engagement (fair-fighting techniques) and a department protocol for managing conflict and solving problems.

- Provide the appropriate amount of autonomy and control, allowing employees to organize and direct their activities. Focus on results.

- Celebrate individual and group success. Look for ways to have fun.

- Develop a learning culture. Support, recognize and hold employees accountable for continuous learning.

- Remain engaged. Be there for employees.

- Role model the attitudes and behaviors expected in others.

- Demonstrate your enthusiasm and optimism. Maintain a sense of humor and a benign amusement to avoid burnout.

- Stay focused on your organization's mission, vision and values. Link them to department-specific standards.

- Remind employees that while you will facilitate their success, they are ultimately responsible for their career choices. They are not powerless or victimized by their particular work frustrations.

- Hold all employees accountable for their work and service ethic, intrinsic motivation, positive attitude and constructive behaviors.

REFERENCES

Buckinham, M. & Coffman, C. (1999). *First, break all the rules: What the world's greatest managers do differently.* New York: Simon & Schuster.

Chambers, H. (1998). *The bad attitude survival guide.* New York: Perseus Books.

Cooperrider, D., Sorenson, P., Whitney, D. & Yaeger, T. (1999). *Appreciative inquiry: Rethinking human organization toward a positive theory of change.* Champaign, IL: Stipes Publishing.

Covey, S. (1989). The seven habits of highly effective people. New York: Simon & Schuster.

Gini, A. (2000). *My job, my self: Work and creation of the modern individual.* New York: Routledge.

Goleman, D. (2000). *Working with emotional intelligence,* New York: Bantam Books.

Spence, G. (1996). *How to argue & win every time: At home, at work, in court, everywhere, everyday.* New York: St. Martins Press.

Stone, D., Patton, B. Heen, S. & Fisher, R. (1999). *Difficult conversations: How to discuss what matters most.* New York: Penguin Books.

Topchik, G. (2001). *Managing workplace negativity.* New York: American Management Association.

ABOUT MICHAEL HENRY COHEN

Mike Cohen is a nationally recognized workshop leader and consultant specializing in leadership and team development, organizational communications, employee relations, conflict management and customer service. He has taught Interpersonal Communications, Group Process and Organizational Behavior at Northwestern, Roosevelt and Dominican Universities, and conducts leadership effectiveness programs for organizations throughout the United States.

Mike served as Director of Employee Relations and Development and Vice President of Human Resources at Weiss Memorial Hospital, Chicago, for 12 years. He holds a Master of Arts degree in Communication Studies from Northwestern University. He is the author of numerous articles and two previous books, *On-the-Job Survival* and *The Power of Self Management*.

Information on Michael H. Cohen's management and employee development workshops can be obtained by perusing his web page, www.michaelhcohenconsulting.com, or by writing to:

Michael H. Cohen
333 N. Euclid Avenue • Oak Park, IL 60302
708.386.1968 • canoepress@yahoo.com